# Message Dimensions of
# Television News

# Message Dimensions of Television News

Robert Shelby Frank

A Foreign Policy Research Institute Book

**Lexington Books**
D.C. Heath and Company
Lexington, Massachusetts
Toronto          London

**Library of Congress Cataloging in Publication Data**

Frank, Robert Shelby.
    Message dimensions of television news.

    (Foreign Policy Research Institute book)
    1. Television broadcasting of news–United States. 2. Television in poli-
tics–United States. I. Title.
PN4888.T4F7       384.55'4'0973       73-8791
ISBN 0-669-90274-8

Published simultaneously in Canada.

Printed in the United States of America.

International Standard Book Number: 0-669-90274-8

Library of Congress Catalog Card Number: 73-8791

To my mother who watches only the news

# Contents

# List of Figures

# List of Tables

# Preface

The genesis of this study can be traced to a meeting of the Research Council of the Foreign Policy Research Institute in May 1971. At that time the subject of the message content of television newscasts had become a matter of national political concern. The issue had become quite controversial with charges and countercharges being hurled back and forth between the Nixon administration and the major networks. Although the subject had been studied by several individuals and groups, we were concerned that the lack of methodological objectivity weakened or rendered nonscientific the conclusions of these previous studies.

May 1971 was a month in the immediate aftermath of the Cambodian invasion. The concern of this institute was in the manner in which TV newscasts affected public attitudes toward foreign policy in general and major events such as the Cambodian invasion in particular. Only after we had begun our research design did it become apparent that it was impossible to separate the foreign policy aspects of the newscast from the reporting of domestic events because the amount of time devoted to "foreign" versus "domestic" was in fact a characterization of the broadcast which might possibly have influenced public attitudes.

Several months were devoted to exploring appropriate ways to tackle this problem. Many useful ideas developed by members of the Research Council and the institute staff were made available and developed by Neal Cutler, the original research coordinator of this project. Cutler also conducted an extensive survey of available literature during the summer of 1972 so that by the fall of that year work could be initiated on a small pilot project. The pilot project was finished in June 1972. The methodologies found most useful were incorporated and further developed during the research conducted on seven weeks of broadcasts recorded on videotape beginning in July 1972 and continuing until the eve of the presidential election.

Our data clearly show that there is wide news-reporting diversity,[a] both among and within networks over different message dimensions and news topics. Even if such diversity had not been found, it would still be debatable whether the American political and social system would be better served either by "de-centralization" of the television news industry or by further government involvement in mass-media affairs, (e.g., through activities such as Federal Communications Commission license review, Office of Tele-Communication

---

[a]Given the exploratory nature of this research, that is, the task of simply outlining previously unexamined message dimensions, given the relative smallness of the news-message sample, and given the fact that no model or inferences concerning news-encoding behavior are presented in this study, "statistical significance" and intervariable correlations will not be presented. Terms such as "wide diversity" are qualitative, normative descriptions which the reader can accept or reject depending upon one's own criteria and/or reading of the tabularly displayed data.

Policy's cable television decisions, and recent satellite communications policies). While this study does not address itself to these political, philosophical, and legal questions, it is hoped that our findings here will present a more accurate picture of the characteristics of television news and thus allow interested groups to approach these fundamental political questions with greater understanding of the nature of television news and its broadcast messages.

Many intellectual and personal debts must be acknowledged to individuals and organizations who made this research possible. The support of the Foreign Policy Research Institute, its Director William R. Kintner, its Deputy Director Robert L. Pfaltzgraff, Jr., and a number of staff personnel (especially Walter F. Hahn, Gerald West, and Ann Lesch, all of whom made valuable contributions to this study at one stage or another) cannot be too gratefully acknowledged. Donna L. Brodsky, without whose advice and assistance this report might never have seen the light of day, is due a special measure of thanks.

The coding staff, Judith Messina, Dick McKee, Dennis Buki, and Melani Lamond, did double duty not only in generating the data but also in closely reviewing this report in its final stages of publication. I could not have asked for a more qualified research team. Gene O'Malley, who handled organizational and financial arrangements during this research, brought some semblance of order where often there was near-confusion, and Robert Herber also facilitated research and offered suggestions at crucial stages in this project. Their help is deeply appreciated. Finally, I wish to thank Kathy Wainwright who accepted the lion's share of the responsibility for putting earlier drafts of this book into manuscript form.

The entire intellectual thrust of this research is indebted to earlier work of Neal Cutler and Albert Tedesco. The brilliant insights contributed by these scholars were invaluable. Large intellectual debts are also owed to David C. Schwartz of Rutgers University, James Murphy of the Annenberg School of Communications, and Robert Meadow of the University of Pennsylvania Political Science Department.

In one way or another, all of the individuals named above deserve credit as coauthors of this report, although I am personally responsible for any errors or shortcomings still remaining in this publication.

Finally, I would like to acknowledge the insight and understanding of the various individuals at the major television networks with whom I have had the honor to be associated. The men and women who are in the business of editing network news have my deepest respect. I hope this report will not only inform the interested readership but will also "ring true" to the practicing news processors insofar as it examines what network news is "all about."

# Message Dimensions of
# Television News

# 1

# Politics and Communication

## Introduction

It is a basic assumption ~~of this study~~ that the analysis of the televised message itself is necessary to a complete understanding of television's role in society. Without prior adequate description of the form and substance of communication, studies dealing with the impact of communication or with the process of encoding by the source must be that much weaker and less accurate.

The characterization of the form and substance of a given televised communication, however, is a somewhat complex affair involving the description of many different components of the televised message. For example, on weekday evenings during the middle of the 1972 presidential campaign, both ABC and NBC broadcast their evening news in the Philadelphia area at 6:30 P.M. CBS followed with a 7 P.M. broadcast to the same market. Thus a viewer with moderate interest in the news could watch one or two presentations of the day's news via the network evening-news format, while a viewer with less interest or time had a choice between two half-hour time slots.

On one sample day ABC's lead story (first story of the broadcast) was the signing of the SALT Agreements by President Nixon. CBS's lead story was an F-111 crash in Indochina. CBS gave extensive background coverage to this story, reviewing the cost-overruns, the broken promises, and the waste involved in production.

NBC's lead story was about the report on Congress issued by Ralph Nader's research team, giving detailed coverage of the Nader charge that Congress was controlled by the executive branch and by big business. The Nader story closed with a field report in which the reporter stated that there was probably no chance of congressional reform in the near future. On NBC, this story was immediately followed by an editorial by David Brinkley who noted, among other things, that the only reason Congress "works" as well as it does is because the United States is rich enough to pay for the "waste" and "extravagance" caused by big-business pressure on Congress. The editorial was followed by a commercial, thus segmenting the story and the editorial as the "lead items" in the evening's news. ABC did not even report the Nader story until well past the midway point of the broadcast, and the ABC editorial was not about congressional reform but instead about television commercials. CBS did not report the Nader story until well into the evening's broadcast, and Eric Sevareid's editorial did not deal with congressional reform but with changing European values in an era of material prosperity.

1

NBC did not cover the SALT Agreements, the lead story on ABC, until almost the end of its broadcast (6:52 P.M.). The entire first half of the NBC broadcast for the evening dealt mostly with two stories: (1) the Nader report on congressional corruption, and (2) the war in Indochina and the tragedy on the *Newport News.*

CBS's third story told of the Patman Committee's attempt to reopen the Watergate investigation. NBC and ABC did not cover this major CBS story until after the midway point in their broadcasts. On CBS there was an interview with Patman, which featured a strong condemnation of White House influence. Non-voice-over film presented the committee's heated discussion, the charges, and countercharges. ABC used similar non-voice-over film and called the hearings a "parliamentary sideshow." The concluding ABC field report said that only continued public interest in the issue could produce an investigation before the election. CBS noted that the only chance for a preelection investigation was the Kennedy Senate subcommittee. NBC gave only a brief verbal report of the story, with John Chancellor covering this event from the studio.

NBC presented an extended "soft news" story (an item of general interest not concerning an event of the day) on the leniency of the Ann Arbor, Michigan marijuana laws, ending with an interview of an Ann Arbor councilman who favored such leniency. The marijuana story was not reported by either of the other two networks that evening. ABC covered stories in which (1) Palestinian guerrillas agreed to leave Lebanon, (2) Indira Gandhi claimed there was CIA influence in India, and (3) the House Ways and Means Committee voted a tax break for parents who pay private-school tuition. None of these stories were broadcast by either of the other two networks. CBS offered a story in which the Senate killed the chances for welfare reform in the immediate future, but this story was not dealt with by ABC or NBC.

Although all networks reviewed the day's political activities of McGovern and Agnew, their coverage differed. ABC showed McGovern campaigning in Boston, "breathing fire," in the words of the reporter. He was seen responding to a heckler, after which shots of a large cheering crowd were shown. Agnew in Indiana was shown on film condemning the "bleeding hearts" who have no sympathy for the people of South Vietnam, and the field reporter observed that the new image of a quiet Agnew is "fading" as he is confronted by hecklers first in Tampa and then in Fort Wayne.

CBS viewed McGovern first walking among the voters, during which his reform proposals were superimposed on the candidate-with-voters film. Film was also shot from behind McGovern revealing a large crowd. The CBS story on Agnew included a distant shot of him speaking, a large but silent crowd, and a review by the candidate of the history of the war in which he did not use any strong political rhetoric. CBS began the Agnew story (after the McGovern coverage) with the statement that "again it was Agnew, not Nixon, who replied."

NBC's coverage of McGovern began with a very tight (close) shot of his face and neck, apparently filmed by a cameraman in the car with the candidate. The concluding field report was filmed in front of a cheering, enthusiastic crowd. Agnew, on the other hand, was shown with a more restrained crowd, and the airtime duration of the crowd film was somewhat shorter. Again, film pictured Agnew calling his hecklers "bleeding hearts," and accusing them of "tearing your country apart." The concluding field report for the Agnew story was shot against the background (unlike the McGovern field report) of an empty airport runway.

This example from one evening's network news typifies the multiple dimensions of news communication on which a given story or series of stories can differ. Such a wide menu of political and social viewpoints indeed increases the amount of information the television viewer has at his disposal. However, if patterns of news reporting can be identified with certain television network news staffs, the further question must be raised as to the effect of habitual viewer utilization of a specific network as a primary source of news. Moreover, the question of overlapping telecasting as a form of network competition in a given market area raises the issue of market differences in the availability of news. Table 1-1 shows the time slots in which the three major network evening news broadcasts appear in eighteen large American cities, as well as the overlap in their presentation. For example, New Yorkers, who can choose to watch only one of the network broadcasts since they are all presented during the same time period, may be said to have less access to national network news than Los Angeles residents who, because of multiple and staggered broadcasts, have at least the possibility of watching all three network news programs in the same evening.

Without the widespread use of domestic videotape facilities (assuming that such facilities would be used if they were available), the possibility of biased network-news orientations exists derived from network-specific characteristics.

What we attempted to do in our research was to explore those different dimensions of the broadcast message within which we felt that some interissue, internetwork encoding differences might appear. While this analysis examined some hitherto underemphasized aspects of the television news message, its descriptive nature and exploratory status suggested that rigid statistical tests could be eschewed at this stage. Especially given the extensive numbers of possible "gatekeepers" and encoding processes that occur prior to airtime broadcast (see Figure 1-1), and given the limits of data in that we restricted ourselves only to the "final product" (the images that appeared on the television screen), the suggestive nature of many of our findings should promote other large-scale and "hypothesis testing" research efforts.

The Foreign Policy Research Institute became involved in the study of political communications and especially in the field of television and politics as a direct outgrowth of a number of ongoing intellectual and research concerns. Information is politically important, in terms of the changing attitudes toward

**Table 1-1**

**Availability Times and Overlap of Early Evening Network News Broadcasts in Major U.S. Cities by City, by Network**

| City | ABC | CBS | NBC | Overlap[c] |
|------|-----|-----|-----|---------|
| Atlanta ( *Constitution*[a] ) | 6:30 | 6:30 | 7 | 1 |
| Boston ( *Globe* ) | 6, 6:30[b] | 6:30[b] | 7 | 0 |
| Chicago ( *Tribune* ) | 5:30 | 5:30 | 6 | 1 |
| Denver ( *Post* ) | 5 | 6 | 5 | 1 |
| Des Moines ( *Register* ) | 5:30 | 5:30 | 5:30 | 2 |
| Cleveland ( *Plain Dealer* ) | 6, 6:30[b] | 6:30 | | 0 |
| Detroit ( *News* ) | 6:30 | 6:30 | 6:30 | 2 |
| Indianapolis ( *Star* ) | 6:30 | 7 | 7 | 1 |
| Los Angeles ( *Times* ) | 5, 5:30, 7[b] | 6:30, 7[b] | 6, 7[b] | 0 |
| Miami ( *Herald* ) | 6, 6:30[b] | 6:30 | 6:30, 7[b] | 0 |
| Minneapolis ( *Tribune* ) | 5:30 | 5:30 | 5:30 | 2 |
| Louisville ( *Courier-Journal* ) | 6 | 6:30 | 6:30 | 2 |
| New Orleans ( *Times Picayune* ) | 6(?) | 5:30 | 5:30 | 1 |
| Philadelphia ( *Bulletin* ) | 6:30 | 7 | 6:30 | 1 |
| Raleigh ( *News and Observer* ) | 6:30 | 6:30[b] | 6:30[b] | 2 |
| St. Louis ( *Post Dispatch* ) | 5 | 5:30 | 5:30 | 1 |
| New York ( *Times* ) | 7 | 7 | 7 | 2 |
| Washington ( *Post* ) | 7 | 7 | 6:30 | 1 |

[a]Denotes newspaper data source.

[b]Indicates multiple broadcasts of a network news program in a given city, i.e., program is available on more than one channel, and possibly at more than one time.

[c]An overlap is the presentation of two different network news broadcasts during the same half-hour slot.

1 overlap  = 2 different network broadcasts presented during the same half-hour time slot.
2 overlaps = all 3 network broadcasts presented during the same half-hour time slot.

| $\bar{x}$ Degree of overlap | ABC | CBS | NBC |
|------------------------------|-----|-----|-----|
| (0 = no overlap)<br>(2 = total overlap) | 1.2 | 1.0 | 1.1 |

national priorities in the United States. In the last analysis, people make demands upon those responsible for foreign policy a direct function of the information with which the people are familiar. Television news, a primary source of information, thus plays a crucial role in various aspects of the political process.

Our original efforts in the field of message analysis entailed a detailed examination of a randomly-selected "sample week" of television news for each network as broadcast in 1969. Using in-shop videotape equipment, trained

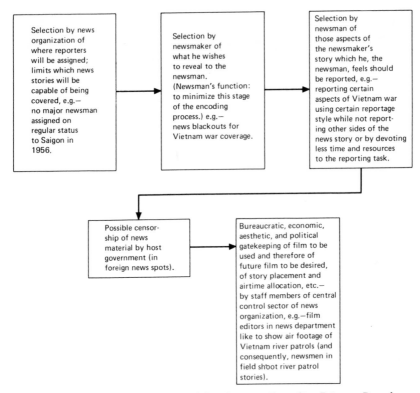

**Figure 1-1.** Examples of Stages of Gatekeeping Encoding Prior to Broadcast Appearance of News Story.

coders, and the able assistance of a number of social scientists, coding protocols were drawn up, message characteristics were initially investigated, much headway was made in learning about the possibilities and problems of human-coder analysis of broadcasted messages, and the groundwork was laid that acts as an intellectual basis for this present monograph. From the findings and experiences with the 1969 data, we felt confident that, even for a presidential campaign year, our techniques and protocols could be directly applied to a multidimensional analysis of message form and content.

Message analysis is a formal exercise in categorizing and describing the shape of the communicated message.[1] The analysis of messages transmitted by television is in itself highly complex. Television broadcasts are multisensory communications which appeal to many levels of feeling and intellect. However, the multidimensional nature of television messages is as yet largely unexplored. It is this very aspect of television's presentation of events which must be studied in order to understand the possible range of variation in television news broadcasts.

Our methodological techniques tap not only the semantic content of television news, but also its visual and format dimensions, especially its use of the "grammar of film." Visual presentation is unique in that it leaves little to the imagination and, more than any other media form, involves the viewer in the here-and-now of an event. Indeed, unlike other forms of mass and person-to-person communication, television more than *reports* the news—it literally *depicts* slices of political and social reality.

While a number of studies have looked at textual and/or allocation of broadcast time to various issues or types of stories, we feel that such a limited approach does not begin to cover the most important and unique characteristic of television, that is, the visual components of the broadcasted message. Rather than simply analyzing the text of the broadcast message (which shares the research orientation of content analysis of print communication) or the airtime allocation of "space" to various issues (which parallels a general strategy of investigation of newspaper content, that is, column-counts), we have made a special effort to examine the "grammar of film" by looking at the visual components of the televised news message.

The actual effects upon specific audiences of this direct presentation of political reality are not empirically explored in this study but will be treated in future supplementary reports and monographs. This chapter discusses the political importance of communications in general and of television news in particular. Thus a general framework of sociopolitical significance is established within which not only the present data but also future data can be considered. This chapter also examines historical examples of the political use of communications and the political importance of changing forms of communication, as well as various components of the communication process and their political effectiveness in television news.

Chapter 2 reviews the development of the methodology of television newscast analysis that we accomplished from mid-1971 to mid-1972 utilizing randomly selected newscasts previously recorded as originally broadcast in 1969. Many of the ideas put forth in Chapter 2 originated in in-shop discussion and internal memoranda (to date unpublished) of members of the research team. Chapter 3 presents the results of our most recent empirical analysis and Chapter 4 is the conclusion. Finally, two appendices are included. Appendix A gives a complete description of the coding protocol used in the campaign-period analysis. Appendix B is the initial questionnaire given to candidates for the coding staff which was recruited for the 1972 campaign-period study.

## Selective Encoding and the
## Nonissue Bias

Before examining the patterns of visual and nonvisual message components, our operational definitions of "news" and of "bias" must be explicated. In terms of political analysis (and it is admitted that this working definition may not hold true for all research into "news"), we are defining *news* as "the events which those who control the communication channels deem worthy of attention and/or 'safe' for the mass audience to know."[2] Thus news is politically important, for it affects men's perceptions of social and political reality and thereby influences their behavior in these spheres.

Control of news and of news sources is obviously a powerful factor in controlling and determining political behavior within a given political system. Leaving aside the long-range implications of the socializing force of mass media, the primary political importance of the channels of communication consists in their role in the dissemination of news:

News is the peripheral nervous system of the body politic, sensing the total environment and selecting which sights and sounds shall be transmitted to the public. More than any other single mechanism, it decides which of the countless billions of events in the world shall be known to the generality of men. Having done so, it alters men's perceptions of the world and of themselves: the more rapid and vivid the communication, the greater this alteration.[3]

Of course television news (or in this case the news-gathering organization) does not and cannot sample the entire surrounding conditions. Receptors respond only to selected modalities of the given environment, and thus in a complete television-news analysis the actual process of news-gathering must be investigated. More importantly, television news cannot transmit all that it has sensed to the "brain," or in this case the mass audiences for news.

The actual channels of television communication contain (they must by definition contain), a series of "gatekeepers" whose role is to determine exactly what, out of all the possible news stories which could be transmitted via television, is indeed newsworthy and deserving of airtime.[4] These gatekeepers must select and choose what will be broadcast. Actual airtime for network evening news ranges from only 19.5 to 24.0 minutes per half-hour broadcast. Given this limited period of time, the gatekeepers must decide what is going to be covered and how extensively. A process of selection and therefore news emphasis is unavoidable. This selection process has been described in one quarter as "the inevitable bias of television."[5] Changing gatekeepers and/or initiating some form of governmental control over the media would not eliminate these biases. It would only result in replacing one form of bias with another. "Bias" implies that a source (or a receiver) is warping, twisting, or needlessly omitting details of information from a message. As we are dealing with an "inevitable bias" resulting from the need to select and report a small body of information from a much larger universe of newsworthy event, we shall hereafter refer to the gatekeeping process in less value-laden terms, that is, by the communications theory description of "selective encoding." In the present report, "selective encoding" looks at the "selected result" of the encoding process. We are looking only at the shape of the television message and the emphases and characteristics of that message. Source characteristics are omitted from this report, as are assumptions concerning the motivations for the selective process the source employs.

The full range of possible sources of inevitable bias cannot even be limited to investigations of the formal source and encoding parameters involved in the message construction and broadcasting or transmitting process. If one wanted to talk about the inevitable biases of network news, one would have to consider not only the biasing influences of the source and socio-economic-political forces behind the news source, one would have to consider the aesthetic, logical, and attributed-significance characteristics of those who edit and transmit the news stories as well as similar characteristics of the various audiences who receive the news messages. This range of possible biasing sources is presented in Table 1-2. Specific cases and tendencies of source bias and audience-response biases will not be empirically studied in this present report. However, the eventual necessity of such research is of course readily apparent.

## The Political Significance of the Communications Process

A full appreciation of the role of communications, and especially televised communication, is best afforded by considering the importance of a political system's communications net for the facilitation of that system's political processes and value-information transfer. While it has been argued that "communication persuades," such a statement is so obviously true that it tends to overshadow the *systemic* importance of communications and especially of television communications. Therefore, a brief discussion of the political-

**Table 1-2**
**Possible Sources of News-Encoder and Audience Bias**

| News Encoder | Audience |
| --- | --- |
| Political values | Political values |
| Peer-group values | Peer-group values |
| Job-career related pressures | Aesthetic norms |
| Aesthetic norms | Educational and family experiences |
| Early educational and family experiences | Information from other news sources |
| Accumulated news-gathering experiences | Situational parameters during news watching |
| | Psychological, economic, and social needs for which the audience member turns to television news to satisfy |

communications interface at the systemic level, as well as an overview of those unique characteristics of televised communication, is in order prior to the presentation of our findings.

Political history as well as the development of certain forms of political organization can, in part, be interpreted as changes in the forms of communications nets, in the political control of these nets, and in the shape of the messages communicated by them. Political action is predicated upon political knowledge. Political motivation is tied to perceived political feasibility. Only through access to the channels of communication can a political force transmit (and a political audience receive) the news of what has been and what is, of what should or will be, or of what can come to pass.

Attempts to influence domestic and foreign opinion through the use of "news" and communication of "newsworthy events" are as old as the history of political organization.[6] Implicit in the control of a communications network is the capability of withholding information. An interesting example of this power is the use of Latin by European political and intellectual elites for 1500 years. As a result, while intrastate elite communication was facilitated, the large majority of Europeans were inadvertently denied knowledge of intellectual, scientific, and political developments. Thus, except for news passed by word of mouth, most Europeans were ignorant of many politically important events of their time. The impact of Gutenberg's printing press and the increased use of vernacular languages helped pave the way for mass-based political power struggles. There is a causal relationship between the opening of the channels of communication in Europe and the development of new forms of state organization and the birth of organized revolutionary activity. The relaxation of the French copyright laws in 1793, the development of the rotary printing press by Koenig in 1813, and the switch from more expensive linen to cheaper wood pulp as the principal ingredient of paper, were developments which increased communication and probably facilitated revolution and sociopolitical change in the nineteenth century. The development and miniaturization of radios and relatively inexpensive broadcast systems in the twentieth century led to the development of elite-mass political linkages, facilitated geographically widespread political organization, and furthered the dissemination of anticolonial rhetoric which helped generate even the Third World political activity of today. As an economic and political elite loses the monopoly of the ability to withhold information, it loses its communication-based political hegemony. As the distribution of political forces having access to the channels of communications changes, profound political reorientations can result.

Franklin D. Roosevelt initiated his Fireside Chats during the late twenties when he was governor of New York in an attempt to reach the upstate voters while circumventing the upstate Republican press. He thus denied that press the political power to withhold or distort information.[7] This circumvention of entrenched print media influence enabled Roosevelt to solidify his New York State power base and allowed him to move onto the national political scene. As a national political leader Roosevelt made similar use of nationally broadcast Fireside Chats to overcome national print media hostility. Thus as in New York, Roosevelt was able to change the national distribution of power and influence through the use of electronic media techniques.

Such control is important to political stability as well as to the attainment of political power. In periods of national crisis, for example, an incumbent regime inevitably attempts to make secure the outlets of communication. When a revolutionary force tries to wrest power from an incumbent government, its first strategic targets inevitably include these same sources of information and opinion. Likewise, in the development of national consciousness and political modernization, control of information outlets by modernizing elites is a *sine qua non* of effective nation-building.[8] In a very real sense, then, the sociopolitical structure of society as well as the legitimized means and ends of government are intimately linked to the shape and control of a national communications network and the messages transmitted within it.[9]

### Review of Research on the Effects of Mass Media

While the effects of mass media have been recognized in Third World contexts, scholars who have dealt with mass-media effects in Western society have, for the most part, minimized the importance of the media as a sociopolitical force.[10] Such a de-emphasis certainly has its own policy implications. We shall not explore these implications here.[11] Rather, we will briefly review some of the major arguments used by those who stress the media's lack of political importance; we will attempt to show that, at least in the case of television news, it is unwarranted to argue that the influence of television news in reinforcing, even shaping, political attitudes and values is minimal.

One argument against the altering effects (as opposed to the reinforcing[12] effects) of mass media is that exposure to any mass medium is, under most conditions, completely voluntary.[13] That use is voluntary is indeed true; yet the inferences that have been drawn from this fact are in large part not valid. Especially in the case of television news, viewing has, in many respects, become *habitual*. Thus, while news watching is "voluntary," this aspect of media use cannot be treated using laws or logical inferences often reserved for the explanation of other (nonhabitual and thus nonequivalent) voluntary behavior. Moreover, while all television use is voluntary, most information receptivity is politically nonselective, that is, liberals watch other than liberal programming and conservatives do not select only conservative informative and persuasive programming.[14] Consequently, the additional argument for a "conservative bias" as fostered by television viewing (in that voluntary watching solely of selected information which reinforces already-held views is by definition a conservative influence) is not valid.

The voluntary and politically nonselective characteristics of media use should clue the researcher to the need to identify specific use of specific media. Blumer and McQuail have shown this to be difficult since (a) in most cases many forms of mass media are used by the news-consumer in a given day, and (b) most "hard news" messages are carried by most or all of the major mass media sources (thus making identification of particular news sources all the more difficult).[15]

The second major argument used in downplaying the importance of the effects of mass media is what has come to be known as the "two-step" model of political influence, which argues that for the nonopinion leaders interpersonal, face-to-face communication is both more pervasive and more influential than information received from a mass-media source.[16] There is firm evidence that a message delivered personally is more persuasive than a written text.[17] Radio (e.g., Kate Smith's war bond drive[18]) and even more so, television, more closely approximate the personal form of communication, at least more than traditional forms of print journalism. Moreover, while there are cultural and even generational differences in attitudes toward mass-media credibility, it may be argued that the generations raised during a period of TV media expansion doubt the validity of these sources, especially television, less than do older generations of printed-mass-media users. These older media users may have more highly developed negative attitudes toward mass-media sources such as radio and newspapers—attitudes which they have in turn transferred to television.

There are specific weaknesses in the two-step model itself. Greenberg has shown that, for the most part, face-to-face communication entails talking to people who the communicator feels are already interested in the given topic of conversation.[19] Moreover, most face-to-face communication, even in a political context, is noncontroversial.[20] Working with the two-step model, it becomes difficult to imagine how mass value and attitude change ever occurs.

Especially in the case of television news, the format has certain characteristics which increase the effectiveness of the medium and which overcome some of the conditions under which the two-step model is most effective. Primarily, television news is seen as a highly credible *information source* and thus the traditional distrust of overt political mass-media messages is reduced. The use of television as a source of information is increasing, while peer-group contacts as a primary source of information are decreasing. For example, 87 percent of the American populace learned of Franklin D. Roosevelt's death by personal communication,[21] whereas only 50 percent of the American people learned of John F. Kennedy's death in this manner.[22] Moreover, those who did learn of Kennedy's death through personal contacts immediately turned to the mass media for more complete information.[23] In fact, according to 1968 statistics, network news broadcasts reached a wider news audience than any other mass-media source;[24] and, more significantly, for the population reached, television was described as the single most important and most credible source of news.

As television news is viewed as raw *information*, the credibility of the news message increases, as many studies of media use for informational purposes have shown.[25] While television must, due to the limitations of the medium, limit the amount of information that can be carried by the channel,[26] the message that does result shapes viewers' personal frames of reference between elections[27] and makes specific issues and candidates more salient during the specific political campaign period.[28]

While face-to-face communication does predominate in the communication of highly important information[29] and/or in the communication of relatively unimportant, target-specific information,[30] television news generally communicates information of moderate political importance,[31] which makes up the great majority of politically significant communication.

In short, we are arguing from two related standpoints that the political effects and importance of mass media, especially television and television news, cannot (or at least should not) be underestimated in attempts to understand the shape and distribution of political values, information, and resultant political power. First, we have argued in the preceding pages that control of sources of information constitutes an effective political tool by which various individuals and groups can either be included in, or excluded from, the societal decision-making process. Moreover, the communication tools by which this information-sharing and transfer process is facilitated have grown in sophistication and effectiveness as a function of increased vividness, speed of transmission, and speed of encoding. In addition, not only does mass communication promise to allow more political groups to gain direct access to the information nexus, but with the advent of television otherwise "nonrepresented" groups can perhaps gain some input to the communication process at least in terms of "making news" and having their positions and political values communicated to large audiences.

Second, we have argued that experimental and quasi-experimental research into mass-media effects is, in many cases, methodologically suspect. Too often these studies have not looked at differing characteristics of communication content, the relationship of content to "news use,"[32] and so forth. Many of these analyses which purport to demonstrate a minimal persuasive influence for mass-media messages have been single-interviews which, by the nature of the research design, could not possibly tap cumulative, longer-range effects.

Controlling for information content and more closely distinguishing between "users" and "inactives" in the opinion-flow process, Troldahl and Van Dam have shown that there are few differences between the opinion givers and the opinion seekers. For the most part, opinion givers are opinion seekers in different contexts:

[P]ersons identified as opinion Givers and opinion Askers . . . were found to be much more similar than earlier studies on public affairs opinion leadership have suggested. They were not significantly different in their exposure to relevant media content, their information level in national news, their occupational prestige, and four or five attributes of gregariousness. . . . [P]ersons who are now categorized as public affairs opinion leaders seem to pass on and compare their opinions on major news topics with persons who are just as active and knowledgeable as themselves.[33]

## Components of Message Effectiveness

The actual extent of the effect of mass media is a function of (1) the size of the audience, (2) the vividness of the message, and (3) the speed of message transmission. National network television news broadcasts represent an enormous maximization of all three of these parameters.

*The Size of the Audience.* One of the important characteristics of television news (as well as other mass media) is that it creates a forum and an audience which can be informed by sources outside the established channels of political authority. At least in a free society, network television news increases the audience that participates, either directly or indirectly, in the political process. Through the coverage of the sensational news event, extralegal and politically marginal political forces can also demand and obtain a quantity and quality of news coverage that they would otherwise be denied. Perhaps the classic example is provided by John Bartlow Martin in his memoirs of the Dominican crisis. Martin recounts one evening at the height of the crisis during which he was watching the evening news:

It appeared that during the afternoon Bonilla Aybar had telephoned German Ornes, publisher of *El Caribe*, from hiding in a friend's house and said that the police had surrounded his own house. He had slipped out of his hideout and into the TV studio and, on his regular 7 P.M. news broadcast, had declared that "they" were after him and that he had asked political leaders and students and labor leaders to come to the studio to help him defend freedom. . . . [I]nside the studio, Bonilla Aybar was hammering away, until suddenly the large arm and then the large back of Belisario Peguero [Commander of the National Police] had come on the screen, blotting out Bonilla, and when the arm and back were gone, so was Bonilla. A moment later the studio was full of politicians, denouncing the police and Bosch, and a man who soon became Bonilla's lawyer, Bienvenido Mejia y Mejia, screamed into the microphone, "Antonio, we need you, only you can save us, otherwise the people will have to take up arms. . . ." [Antonio was Antonio Imbert Barrera, one of the two surviving men who had assassinated Trujillo.]
Station Rahintel was showing a program which seemed to be live, the cameras kept tilting as though being jostled, dozens of people seemed to be milling around, a camera would focus for a minute on Alfonso Moreno of the Social Christians shouting into the microphones, then would abruptly shift to Viriato Fiallo, then to another politician, then to another, then to a man with what seemed to be blood dripping down his shirtfront, then to policemen. It looked as though a riot were going on in the studio.[34]

*Vividness of the Message.* The example of Station Rahintel also illustrates the second power of television and specifically of television news, that is, a heightened vividness of communication unavailable to print journalism. Successful revolutionary forces have been known to drag the dead bodies of leaders of the previously incumbent regime into the television studio to demonstrate convincingly that the revolution has been a success.[35]

The vividness of visual communication afforded by television (a) appeals to sectors of the audience who either cannot read, cannot read well, or who do not read as a habit, thereby increasing the scope of the participating political actors, and (b) adds a sense of reality and credibility which a printed or even an audio message cannot begin to match. With the development of inexpensive and miniaturized projection systems that can broadcast holographic images, the importance of the vividness of the news message will increase exponentially. Instead of seeing a war, a riot, a press conference, a national convention, three-dimensional holographic projection will allow the news viewer, for all intents and purposes, to be at the battle scene, in the riot, participating in the press conference, on the floor of the convention.

The vividness of television news adds to its credibility as an information source. As recently as late August 1972, an Opinion Research Corporation poll found that with a nationwide probability sample, 63 percent of the respondents felt television was most complete in its news reporting, while only 19 percent selected newspapers, 7 percent favored magazines, and only 5 percent chose radio. In the same survey, 53 percent of the sample felt television was the most objective source of news, while newspapers ran a distant second with 15 percent of the sample. The other sources of news lagged even further behind. The most startling results of this survey came when the question was asked, "When you feel that TV political bias does exist, what direction do you feel it takes?" Fully one-third of the respondents had no opinion, that is, they were apparently unable to discern enough bias in television news to be able to identify the direction that such bias was taking.[36] The vividness and seeming completeness of television news may blind the audience to existing network selection processes and thus act as powerful factors in the effective communication of the message.

*Speed of Transmission.* The third element that contributes to the political power of television news, the rapidity of transmission, has also made enormous inroads in cutting the lag-time of news reporting. Near-instantaneous reporting of news events from one area of a political system to large numbers of people throughout the system, especially when such reporting is not routed through governmental news-gatekeepers, can create severe strains and bring unexpected pressures to bear on the governmental structure. The reporting of the Martin Luther King assassination in 1968, which led to immediate nationwide urban rioting, caught federal, state, and local governmental units unprepared and unable to cope with, or establish buffers against, the massive civil disorder and destruction of property.[37]

Rapidity of transmission time is, in turn, a function of two variables: (a) the speed of transmission and (b) the speed of encoding. The transmission speed for news has increased fantastically.[38] With the development of instantaneous worldwide communication through the use of communication satellites and directly broadcastable videotape, there is potentially no lag-time between an event happening anywhere on the globe and the knowledge of that event by the rest of the world's population. The implications of this speed of transmission, as well as the fact that "jamming" such satellite communications is practically impossible,[39] have serious ramifications for international politics. At the very least, we can agree with Fred Friendly's observation that "satellites promise to change television as much as television altered radio."[40] This change in capabilities and political import is a function of the speed of communication.

Contemporary television, and therefore television news, also enjoys a near-instantaneous speed of encoding. One of the factors influencing the speed at which a news event can be communicated to large audiences is the time it takes to "put the message together" prior to transmission. Semaphore signals, an early form of communication which did possess rapid transmission speed over short distances, suffered due to the slowness of encoding time.[41] Letterpress printing was able to reach larger audiences (although not as instantaneously) while cutting encoding time to approximately one line of print per minute. Linotype machines cut the encoding time to 4.9 lines per minute, the Teletypesetter after 1932 cut the encoding time to 5.6 lines per minute, while computerized typesetting raised the typesetting speed to 14 lines per minute. In 1967 a CBS-Mergenthaler Linotron was put into operation by the U.S. Government Printing Office. Using optics and electronics instead of lead casting, the Linotron casts fifteen thousand lines a minute. As Bagdikian notes, "The Bible, whose letters took Gutenberg five years to set, could now be produced by the Government Printing Office in twenty-seven minutes—once the programmers had created the magnetic tape to instruct the computer how to project the letters onto the page."[42]

Rapid as this encoding might be, it is still far slower than the electronic and film resources that are available to television news. Film, theoretically, is "encoded" as quickly as the time it takes for the photosensitive chemicals on the film to set. Yet, film entails processing and editing time of minutes, sometimes hours for large quantities of film, in order to retrieve the encoded images from the film. Videotape requires no processing time whatsoever. Television cameras can electronically record a news story, send that signal directly to a satellite (through an adequate beaming system, of course) where the signal is bounced back to earth, amplified, and broadcast immediately to the audience.[43]

Thus, in terms of the three elements of a communicated message, the speed of transmission, the vividness of the message, and the size of the audience, television and especially television news emerges as the most powerful communication force in American political life. Indeed, the news has created what Joseph Klapper has called the "news addict" who is characterized by "an ardent hunger which is sated by the five-minute newscast, despite its lack of detail and regardless of its irrelevance to the addict's life and interests."[44] Television news has become a "habit."[45] It is *the* source of information about political reality for millions of Americans. The news is vivid, it is immediate, and it is all-pervasive. The news that is broadcast by television in the global arena is even more politically significant. In a world in which 55 percent of all Asians and 82 percent of all Africans are illiterate (1960 UNESCO figures), the potential power of audio and visual programming can hardly be ignored by scholars of political behavior at any level of analysis.

## Politicians and the News

One of the messages transmitted by mass-media sources is that of political images. Given the pervasiveness and significance of television in modern society, we can expect this medium to foster a new breed of political elites who will not only adapt to the requirements of television presentation, but also exploit its advantages and uniqueness in order to achieve political success. In fact, one who does not so adapt may face political failure as in the case of William Jennings Bryan during the 1924 Democratic National Convention. This convention was one of the first to be broadcast to the nation over radio. Bryan, as planned, was at his "Cross of Gold" best. Yet, he could not refrain from storming around the stage as he harangued the delegates. Consequently, he continually walked out of receiving range of the radio microphone. Only snatches of his politically rousing speech were heard by the radio audience.[46]

Bryan was ill-suited to "make" radio news because of his personality as well as his past political training. In America today most rising political figures owe their success in large part to their adaptability to television. Broadcast images influence the entire shape of the contemporary elite membership. McGinniss,[47] Nimmo,[48] and others[49] have shown the power of television as a campaign resource in determining political success (although access to the media in itself cannot guarantee this success). Television coverage seems to be a necessary but not sufficient component of a successful political campaign. And, due to the unique problems television has in holding its audience,[50] it tends to cover the glamorous and controversial, thus emphasizing certain personalities and certain realities of political life.

Perhaps the most important segment of possible television coverage is the candidate coverage afforded by the network evening news. Mendelsohn and Crespi note that "one of the prime reasons that presidential candidates go scooting about the country is simply to provide footage for both local and national television newscasts."[51] Robert Kennedy, it has been reported, felt that thirty seconds on the network evening news was worth more than political coverage in a story in every newspaper in the world.[52] As Abraham J. Multer, a Congressman from the Thirteenth Congressional District of New York, admits:

The more a public figure is in the news, attracting the public's attention, the more his actions are reported to the people through the medium of television, the more indelibly impressed are the viewers with the name, the face, and especially the value of that figure.[53]

Yet, for the most part (and contrary to the assertions of some television industry representatives[54]), office seekers and the news they make, as well as the coverage of the more general political issues of the day, does not simply get "reported" by the television news. The 1960 Kennedy-Nixon debates offer a prime example. It is generally agreed that Kennedy "won" the first of the 1960 television debates. The second debate, which was held in the NBC studios, was more "loaded" in favor of Nixon. The vice-president convinced NBC to cool the studio to 60° (to offset his tendency to perspire and thereby look nervous). Moreover, as John Kennedy walked on to the stage to inspect and try out his chair, he noticed that he would have four studio lights shining in his face while Nixon would have only one. As Kennedy remarked: "When I saw all those lights, I decided that NBC had chosen its candidate."[55]

This chapter has reviewed the role of mass media and especially television as a political phenomenon. Those characteristics of the communication process that are politically significant have been discussed. In short, it has been argued that:

1. Channels of communication, their shape and their control, are vitally important political instruments.
2. Limiting the size and/or scope of an audience by withholding information or by denying access to the use of communications channels and by controlling the news reporting lag-time are two potentially powerful political weapons.
3. Television news shapes domestic attitudes, may reshape national political systems, and generates a new, media-attractive breed of political elites.
4. In a four-stage model of communicated influence, the analysis of transmitted messages is crucial for the description, analysis, and understanding of the entire communications process.
5. Message effectiveness in a communications system is a function of the size of the audience, the vividness of the message, and the speed of message transmission.
6. Television news maximizes each of the above politically significant factors of communication.
   a. Television news by the vividness of its message adds a sense of credibility and objectivity (which may not in fact exist) to the transmitted message.
   b. The political effectiveness of television reporting is a result of (1) practically eliminating encoding time and (2) maximizing message transmission speed.

# 2

## Developing Techniques of Television Content Analysis

### Introduction

Chapter 2 of this report will discuss the issues involved in content analysis of network television news, how we became interested in these issues, and some of the techniques that are available in the content analysis of television news. Those techniques we used in a 1969 pilot study will be briefly discussed and the strengths and weaknesses of these approaches will be reviewed. The interrelationships among the data sets generated using the 1969 techniques will be considered and some general network characteristics which were found will be reviewed. The 1969-data pilot-study techniques will then be compared with the techniques used in the 1972 study to show the complementarity of these different content analytic strategies. Finally, Chapter 2 will conclude with a thumbnail sketch of our 1972 coding staff and with a review of the content-analytic categories these coders used in the 1972 content-analytic tasks.

Beginning in June 1971 the Foreign Policy Research Institute conducted a study designed to measure bias, if any, objectively in the nightly national television news broadcasts of the three principal networks. We originally began this analysis because of our concern that inaccurate or biased TV reporting of news concerning foreign affairs could adversely affect support of the United States government's foreign and national security policies. The Foreign Policy Research Institute has long been interested in the domestic sources of demands upon foreign policymakers,[1] and the review presented in the preceding section highlights the importance of television news as one of the prime sources of attitudes and values which constitute that domestic input into the foreign-policy process.[2] As our study progressed, however, it became apparent that one could only analyze the foreign-policy news reporting within the context of the entire newscast.

During the process of our investigation we examined a variety of prior efforts that have been made to measure the objectivity of national TV newscasts as well as network defense of the objectivity of their news presentations. We found that both the critics and defenders of these news broadcasts relied on modes of analysis that were more characterized by subjective attitudes than empirical evidence. We endeavored, therefore, to establish an empirical basis for analyzing the bias, if any, in national news broadcasts.

At the onset, we decided to confine our investigation to what came out of the television tube and were not concerned with the motivation or behind-the-scenes decisions that led to a particular news broadcast. Nor initially were we concerned with the effect of the broadcast upon the voters, although there is an abundance of existing communications research documenting the overriding importance of television as a source of politically-relevant information for many sectors of the mass public.

After we had carefully constructed a research design that would achieve our purposes, we undertook a pilot test study of five *randomly drawn* weekdays of 1969, each day represented by videotapes of all three network broadcasts supplied by the recently established Television Network News Archive at Vanderbilt University. From our pilot study we became convinced of the feasibility of accurate, objective, and intellectually sound content analysis of television news. The components of this analysis include: (1) data from the television "logs," (2) the use of human coders to investigate manifest broadcast dimensions, (3) the application of kinesic audio and visual analysis techniques to ascertain the underlying latent broadcast dimensions, and (4) the development of applicable computer techniques for the realization of "perfect reliability" content analysis of newscast transcripts.

### Issues in the Content Analysis of Network Television News

Our initial efforts were devoted to looking at the simple distribution of news stories during the evening news broadcasts according to the various areas of the international environment which were thus reported. Leaving aside for the moment questions of within-broadcast emphasis (e.g., story placement within the evening's news reports), the first effort of the Foreign Policy Research Institute was a simple mapping operation of various stories along two criteria: (1) did the news story deal with foreign events, that is, with stories which occurred in, or related to, specific non-American areas of the world, and (2) if the answer to the first question was affirmative, which areas of the world were covered in the news story? A review of this technique is provided by Cutler in an early working paper from this project:

The first question within each part simply asked if the news item had a particular attribute, e.g., Does the item involve the Middle East? Does the item involve the U.S. armed forces? Does the item involve the relations between the United States and another country? If the answer to such a question was negative, the coder went on to the next question in the series. If the answer was positive, a second question would be asked, e.g., What country or countries are the focus of the Middle East story? Does the story involve the draft or overseas activities of the armed forces? What other country is the object of the relationship with the United States?

Thus each news item is represented by a series of attributes which in turn represent a substantive question. Attributes and answers need only be recorded when the answer to the first question in the pair is positive. Absence of the attribute implies a negative answer to the question "Does this news item involve X?" (Neal E. Cutler, "Methodological Aspects of Content Analysis of Television Videotaped Materials," Philadelphia: Foreign Policy Research Institute, 1970.)

While such an approach can give a rough approximation of the various areas of the world being covered in the network evening news, it overlooks two important dimensions. First, it is not possible through such a simple frequency count to analyze the various and often competing aspects or dimensions of the news message in which different amounts of encoding emphasis can be placed. Second, a mapping of the presence of various international areas of the world on the network evening news does not come to grips with the question of what is *not being reported.*

This second problem is a major theoretical issue and one that compelled our research group to move toward a complete analysis of all the stories appearing in the network evening news. These evening news broadcasts must, by the simple fact of making salient various issues and news stories, in some way set the "agenda" for the country in the sense of communicating to the audience "what is important." This is recognized by Cobb and Elder in their study of agenda setting:[3] "The mass media plays a pivotal role in highlighting this interplay [between issues and symbolic communication] and in determining the success of an issue.[4] As Norton Long has written, "To a large extent, it [the press] sets the civic agenda."[5]

This pivotal role is also played by the electronic mass media of network television news. In both print journalism and in electronic journalism, one of the most powerful influences on the shape of the agenda is the limitations of what gets included in that agenda. Newspapers are constrained in terms of what they will or can report as a function of the amount of advertising that they have to fill up a page. As Bagdikian writes:

Those who handle the flow of advertising into the daily editions are important because, among other things, they determine how much space will be left for news. On almost all papers the advertising department determines the total pages to be printed and only after this does news receive its allocation.[6]

A similarly effective limitation exists for television news in terms of the airtime allotted for the news. The ultimate or final limitation for the allocation of airtime for news and for newspapers is primarily economic (i.e., the necessity to get sponsors who are willing to pay for certain types of programming at specific hours or half-hours of the evening).[7] For the day-to-day reporting of significant occurrences of the sociopolitical world, airtime and newsprint economic limitations do exist, as well as the political (editorial) policies which in themselves determine the shape of the news and the fate of specific political issues which do, or do not, make the national agenda.

While the present study looks only at the actual news broadcasts presented during the traditional dinner hour, the notion of limited airtime or limited newspaper space can be somewhat offset by an analysis of supplementary news programs from nondinnertime standard news broadcasts. It is the case that given a limited amount of time, certain aspects of the political world can "swamp" the news format in that the newsworthiness of these events must be reported. For example, if there were significant developments in the Vietnam war, these developments would eat up much of the available news time. Now, if there is a major earthquake in San Francisco or widespread urban rioting and burning, these domestic events must be covered. The danger of this swamping effect is the greatest when the news story is important enough to capture most of the available news time but not important enough to warrant a special half-hour or hour program devoted to this newsworthy event. In the latter case, when the event is of a requisite degree of importance, the swamping effect either levels off or is sometimes reduced by the news tactic of announcing a later special on the news topic and moving on to other news items on the reporting agenda. A concurrent analysis of the types of content of news specials and programs, along with the frequency of these specials, would be a valuable research effort in measuring the nature and dimensions of this flooding, limited newstime effect. Such research has yet to be undertaken.

In addition to the possibility of looking at nonevening news specials, the handling of possible swamped news broadcasts can be accomplished through the expansion of the data set. A thorough content analysis of the network news with the aim of looking at the coverage of foreign affairs must include an analysis of all the news stories appearing in the news programs, and such analysis should be longitudinal, that is, be executed over a relatively long period of time. Thus possible short-lived, highly significant news stories which appear in a more limited sample of network news and which innundate specific newscasts will not seriously distort the data, the findings, and the implications to be drawn from the study. Random sampling within a longer period, moreover, will guarantee against "continued stories" which may occur over all the days of a smaller news sample.

A related problem in the analysis of foreign news coverage and in the importance attributed to the international arena by the network evening news broadcasts deals with the difficulty of adequately distinguishing between those stories which are "foreign" and those stories which are "domestic." The problem is a two-fold one. On the one hand, certain aspects of foreign-affairs stories have very strong domestic news or domestic issues components. On the other hand, in the eyes of the viewers, as with any other individual or group who is being informed, certain priorities must be established between broad scopes of governmental activities and issues. By definition, the salience of either foreign or domestic issues, even if both are covered in approximately the same manner, must in large part occur at the de-emphasis of the other. The phenomena of "symbolic saturation" and "urgency portent" as discussed by Cobb and Elder[8] come into play to give a value or salience hegemony to specific types of issues to the devaluation and de-emphasis of other types of issues. It is assumed that the domestic-foreign dichotomy is most available as a cognitive categorization operation of the news audiences.

In terms of maintaining a valid distinction between foreign and domestic news stories as they appear in the evening news, perhaps the most difficult news-issue areas relate to military research and development, possible cost overruns, domestic labor demands and/or disputes (e.g., the refusal to unload specific cargo from specific foreign nations), and the like—and a parallel set of concerns relating to the area of finance and macroeconomics (tariff laws and proposed changes therein, wheat deals with the Soviet Union, and so forth). For the most part these types of news stories were considered to be domestic stories, and in the foreign-domestic coverage ratios presented in the following section such "linkage politics" (the presence of relationships between foreign and domestic affairs) news stories were coded as domestic stories. Nevertheless, especially in the case of military affairs and to some extent in the commercial and financial worlds, closely defined distinctions were drawn between types of news stories (in the case of military-related stories dealing with research and development, cost-overruns, and so forth, all such stories were given a specific category), and double-coding techniques described in detail elsewhere in this report, combined with the closeness or fineness of the various coding categories, has left us with data that can be reaggregated and reanalyzed using other combinatorial principles.

Nevertheless, the very existence of this "gray area of content" between the foreign and the domestic news story types adds further weight to the argument that distinction between foreign and domestic news with a total elimination of the latter cannot adequately explore the patterns, distributions, and broadcast salience of the former.

## Content Analytic Techniques

The content analytic procedures used in the pilot research were developed after prior extensive investigation into alternative methods of content analyzing television news broadcasts. A major decision was whether to use the "hard" or the "soft" approach to content analysis, where the *hard* approach is defined as a simple frequency count of words, seconds or airtime coverage, and other discrete and concrete quantifiable bits of data. The *soft* approach, on the other hand, utilizes the judgment of trained coders to evaluate the entire Gestalt package of the news story, the news segment, and/or even of the entire news broadcast.

The hard approach is most clearly characterized in the content analysis by Stempel of the 1960 coverage of the presidential campaign by the "prestige press" in the United States. Stempel made a simple frequency count of lines, pictures, and so forth.[9] No characteristics of bias in the prestige press were inferred, not only because of the relative balance of the news coverage during the campaign but also because Stempel argued that there was no objective way of ascertaining exactly what the "objective frequency counts" should have been. Nevertheless, the hard approach has been utilized again and again to infer bias, the most popularized version being the study by Efron of general news coverage of the national network evening news.[10]

The soft approach, a more "wholistic" approach to news coverage, was utilized in our research generally in the form of semantic differential coding of various thematic and structural aspects of the evening-news presentations. Certain aspects of the news presentation, such as the effect of combinations of news stories, that is, the structural characteristics of the entire news program, cannot be analyzed using simple frequency counts of message characteristics which appear during each story analyzed specifically. For example, a series of four stories may "set the tone" of a broadcast, may develop a news theme, which will affect the presentation and the reception by the audience of a fifth news story. The fifth story might cover the president's efforts to solve the inflation problems plaguing the economy. If this fifth story is preceded by four stories which report how easily some world leaders have recently solved their own nations' inflation problems, the audience evaluation of Nixon's failure to solve the United States inflation could be quite different than if the same story had been preceded by other types of news stories. For example, Table 2-1 shows two hypothetical newscasts with identical fifth stories but different stories in the first four positions.

Such news-message characteristics of groupings cannot be handled by "hard content analysis" of single stories, and thus early in our research we opted for a coding scheme combining both the hard and the soft approaches. Thus stories could be rated by coders using "soft" content analytic techniques along underlying dimensions of news-stories groups. The soft approach, in which we used the semantic differential techniques, is reviewed by Cutler in a working paper prepared for this project:

Thus one may argue both from a general knowledge of the genre of semantic differential research, that the differential encoding can be empirically measured through the semantic differential technique. The concept or object rated along the series of common scales can be a set of statements chosen from news broadcasts, the name of particular news sources (both institutional and personal), whole news stories, and even viewings of entire news programs. After

### Table 2-1
### Hypothetical Comparison of Two Newscasts

| Newscast A Story # | Newscast B Story # |
| --- | --- |
| 1. Brandt solves inflation problems. | 1. Communist attack on Hue. |
| 2. Trudeau solves inflation problems. | 2. U.S. responds to communist attack. |
| 3. Pompideau solves inflation problems. | 3. War costs are rising. |
| 4. Sato solves inflation problems. | 4. Labor unions demand higher wages. |
| 5. *Nixon tries to solve inflation problems but is having some trouble doing so.* | 5. *Nixon tries to solve inflation problems but is having some trouble doing so.* |

exposure to the stimulus object, the coders record positions on the various scales. The average scale positions for a number of objects then can be compared directly; for example, NBC's semantic differential profile can be compared with CBS' and ABC's. Television news can be compared with newspaper and news magazine news; all may be compared with the profiles generated by phoney news stories which have been purposely written in either biased or quite neutral terms. In his "Communicator Image and News Reception,"[11] for example, Sargent used the semantic differential to compare the ratings given to the same news story when (in an experimental situation) the stated news sources were varied to reflect either personal or institutional sources. He found that the personal news sources were rated more positively on the scales comprising the Ethical dimension, and more calmly on the Activity dimension. (Cutler, "Methodological Aspects")

There are strengths and weaknesses to each approach. In soft-content analysis the possibility always exists that the coders themselves have strong predispositions toward various political issues and that messages presented will be coded not according to the inherent "biases" or sensationalism of the messages but rather as a function of the orientation toward the political issues being reported. Hard-content analysis asks the coders to identify simply discrete bits of message characteristics that appear. The judgmental factor leading to possible coding error is for the most part eliminated. Nevertheless, this trade-off results in the loss of coded information, as described above. The optimal technique, and one which we employed in our research, was the construction of a research design which utilized both forms of content analysis.

### Data Sets and Their Interrelationships

The pilot project resulted in the development of four primary data sets. These were:

1. *TV Logs.* Each program in the sample was viewed by a panel consisting of the principal investigators and staff assistants. The following information was recorded for each program: (a) each news story content type within the program was identified; (b) each news story and component segments were timed; (c) each segment of the news story was identified and labeled according to the amount and type of film resources allocated to its coverage; (d) each news story on the tape was assigned a location number to enable future retrieval and reanalysis; (e) the name of the anchorman and reporter for each story and story segment was noted.
2. *Recording Instrument.* The recording instrument included several distinct sections: (a) a series of foreign-domestic indicators; (b) an inventory of substantive news types; (c) measures of story setting, origin, and location; (d) measures of the presence or absence of critics and spokesmen of the

administration; (e) measures of story type; (f) evaluative measures, in the form of an inventory of semantic differential scales, of the presentation of the issue in the news story (generated for every news story); (g) evaluative measures (semantic-differential scales) of the style of news story presentation of personalities (key individuals) who appeared in the news story.

3. *Kinesic Analysis.* (Analysis of facial behavior patterns and speech rate.) A multidimensional analysis of anchorman audio and kinesic records was developed using traditional psychometric and psycholinguistic techniques. The focus of this data set is the measurement of arousal states and other psychological indices through the assessment of speech rate, rate of delivery, nod and blink rates, and so forth.

4. *Text Analysis.* The application of computer programs and "canned" dictionaries to the transcribed record of program texts was generated. A reliable, machine-coded map of the text of selected programs was generated using concordance (key-word-in-context) programs. (Verbal encoding characteristics of dialogue in interview situations can be analyzed using this procedure.) A cross-network analysis of principal speakers on given issues was also made.

The six indicators were obtained using these four data sets as illustrated in Figure 2-1.

The results of utilizing such a strategy is described by Cutler in his working paper "Methodological Aspects of Content Analysis of Television Videotaped Materials":

The analysis of the data, as described in the preceding sections, will be facilitated by having the measurement indexes and the substantive codes punched onto IBM cards. One card will be prepared for each news item; the punchcard record for each item will also contain, of course, identification data concerning date and network. Quite simple computations will allow us to determine the average amounts of coverage for various news types across the different networks. When converted from minutes into percentage of total news minutes, the television data can be compared with printed media scores obtained when column-inches are also converted to percentages. Although positional variables, such as placement within the news half-hour versus placement on the printed page, may not be directly comparable, we can easily convert such data to rankings within media, and then compare the rankings across media.

The research design will produce a three-dimensional matrix of information, the dimensions representing (1) substantive news categories; (2) measures and indexes of news salience and mode of presentation; and (3) alternative mass news media. Comparisons can then be made in a variety of ways, such as the relative salience given to various substantive categories within and across media. To the degree that a necessary condition for the attribution of bias is the presence of substantial differences in the context or style of news presentations, the approach outlined in this proposal will allow us to determine if bias is potentially present. At this stage, we will have learned a great deal about the dynamics of news presentations in the American mass media. We will then be ready to design subsequent stages of research aimed at the determination of the subjectively perceived differences in the various news presentations. Since we

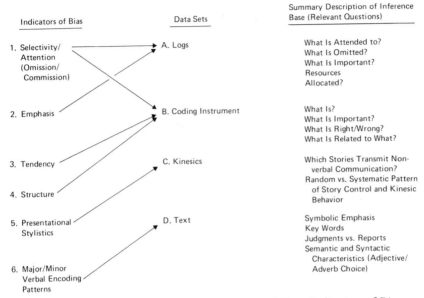

**Figure 2-1.** Flow Diagram of Multiple Streams of Data, Indicators of Bias and Inference Base.

will have maintained our newspaper, magazine, and television news presentations, the very same data which provided the content analyses can be used as the stimulus objects in such behavioral techniques as the semantic differential. When we subsequently determine the interrelationship between objective content characteristics of the messages and the subjectively-perceived attributes of the same messages, we will then be in a position to understand the potential short-term and long-term effects of bias in mass media news presentations. (Cutler, "Methodological Aspects")

Using these techniques, the following network message characteristics were found for a random sample of 1969 network evening news presentations. By network, the appropriate characteristics are listed in Table 2-2.

## Summary and Evaluation of Advantages of Techniques Developed and Used in the 1969 Data Study

The study which used the 1969 data resulted in a series of network characteristics that have been presented in Table 2-2. In addition, a number of specific findings relating to the frequencies and distributions of message content for the sample week of network news that was coded in the 1969 data study are available elsewhere.[12] Before turning to the 1972 data generated during the

**Table 2-2**
**Dominant Characteristics of Network Presentations**

| Measure | Message Characteristic | Table Reference[b] |
|---|---|---|
| **ABC** | | |
| News profile | Most interesting | 8.9 |
| (computer text, | Most interesting, | A.1 |
| semantic differential) | foreign news | |
| | Most balanced, | A.1 |
| | foreign news | |
| Time allocation | Economy, taxes[a] | 7.3 |
| priorities (all stories) | Antiwar movement | 7.3 |
| (TV logs) | Mideast | 7.3 |
| Vietnam emphasis, time | Peace talks[a] | 7.4 |
| allocation (TV logs) | Battlefield operations | 7.4 |
| Sequential allocation | Defense programs[a] | 7.8 |
| emphasis (TV logs) | Vietnam battlefield | 7.8 |
| | operations | |
| Story type and story | Most "soft news" | 6.6 |
| tone (human coder pairs) | Most "light news" | 6.6 |
| **CBS** | | |
| News profile | Most impartial | 8.9 |
| (computer text, | Most complete | 8.9 |
| semantic differential) | Most balanced | 8.9 |
| | Most complex | 8.9 |
| | Most impartial, domestic | A.2 |
| | news | |
| | Most complete, domestic | A.2 |
| | news | |
| | Most balanced, domestic | A.2 |
| | news | |
| | Most complex, domestic | A.2 |
| | news | |
| | "Most wordy" | 10.3 |
| Time allocation | HEW, Consumer | 7.3 |
| priorities (all stories) | affairs[a] | |
| (TV logs) | Antiwar movement | 7.3 |
| | Defense programs | 7.3 |
| Vietnam emphasis, time | Peace talks[a] | 7.4 |
| allocation (TV logs) | U.S. casualties | 7.4 |
| Sequential allocation | Vietnam battlefield | 7.8 |
| emphasis (TV logs) | operations[a] | |
| | Peace talks | 7.8 |
| | Defense programs | 7.8 |
| Story type and story | Most "hard news" | 6.6 |
| tone (human coder pairs) | Most "serious news" | 6.6 |
| **NBC** | | |
| News profile | Most accurate, foreign | A.1 |
| (computer text, | news | |
| semantic differential) | Most complete, foreign | A.1 |
| | news | |

**Table 2-2** (cont.)

| Measure | Message Characteristic | Table Reference[b] |
|---|---|---|
| | Most complex, foreign news | A.1 |
| Time allocation | Defense programs[a] | 7.3 |
| priorities (all | HEW, Consumer | 7.3 |
| stories) (TV logs) | affairs | |
| | Economy, taxes | 7.3 |
| Vietnam emphasis, time | U.S. casualties[a] | 7.4 |
| allocation (TV logs) | Life in Vietnam | 7.4 |
| Sequential allocation | Defense programs[a] | 7.8 |
| emphasis (TV logs) | Intra-Communist affairs | 7.8 |
| | Mideast | 7.8 |

[a]Represents rank ordering of resource allocation emphasis.

[b]Refers to specific table number from N.E. Cutler, A.S. Tedesco, and R.S. Frank, *The Differential Encoding of Political Images* (Philadelphia: Foreign Policy Research Institute, 1972).

presidential election campaign, it is appropriate that we briefly review the strengths and weaknesses of the techniques developed in the prior 1969-data pilot study.

The 1969 analysis utilized a large number of coders who were chosen from a class in mass media and politics taught at the University of Pennsylvania by Dr. Neal Cutler. The financial costs of using a larger number of coders will generally be higher than working with a select few who have been recruited from the academic or classroom community. In addition, the data collection and processing which accompanies the use of a larger number of coders can become both more complex and more costly.

On the other hand, the utilization of a larger number of coders can be a viable alternative strategy to the recruitment techniques and rationales used in the 1972 study. The 1972 study attempted to guarantee thorough yet impartial coding through a rigid selection technique (see Appendix B). In the study conducted in the 1969 data, the thoroughness and *group* impartiality was guaranteed by increasing the numbers of coders used and assigned to each coding task and then aggregating and establishing mean scores across all the coders. The more coders used, the closer the coding staff will come to approximating an entity with normally distributed predispositions, political attitudes, and evaluations of the medium.

Given the availability of necessary financial and technological resources, the optimal strategy would be to utilize both techniques simultaneously. A rigid selection procedure could be used to filter out the extreme cases along political and media-value dimensions. Once the general parameters of coder acceptability were established, the investigators could multiply the number of "moderate" coders and use the aggregation techniques of the 1969 data study. Indeed, in the

1969 data study, a questionnaire was administered to the coders to ascertain orientations and backgrounds along a number of dimensions covered in the questionnaire presented in Appendix B, but in the 1969 data study this questionnaire was used to identify possible sources of consequent biased coding and not to eliminate applicants and select coders from a larger group of potential coding assistants.

Not only were there differences in the coding-staff size and recruiting principles from the 1969 to the 1972 studies, but the investigation of nonverbal behavior of newscasters and the computer analysis of the texts of the newscasts which we conducted during the 1969 pilot project were not used in the 1972 campaign-period study. While the techniques developed using these data sources were shown to discriminate among behavioral responses in presenting the news and among textual components of the news presentations, these techniques, much like the use of multiple coders, were found to be relatively expensive.

Both of these data sources, the nonverbal and textual records, can tell the researcher not only about the shape of the news message that is transmitted to the audiences but also about certain psychological or psychopolitical characteristics of the newscasters themselves. Textual analysis can present information concerning a wide range of personality and psychic state dimensions, dimensions well documented in the literature of psychopolitics and psycholinguistics which is too extensive to even begin to list here.[13] In the case of the pilot project using 1969 data, for example, need-achievement imagery frequencies of network speakers were explored.[14] In our investigation of the nonverbal or kinesic behavior of Walter Cronkite, we also learned something about the rates of arousal that were associated with Cronkite's reporting of different types of news stories.[15]

While it can be expected that such verbal imagery or such nonverbal behavior will be manifested by the newscasters who present the news,[16] in both cases those cues to personal psychological characteristics radiated are picked up and acted upon by audiences or receivers of the psycholinguistic and nonverbal cues.[17] As such, a full-scale, longitudinal analysis of these two data sources, if financially and technologically possible, should be included in an overall battery of message characteristics of network news broadcasts.

There are also subtle differences between the two studies in terms of the relationship between the coding staff and the principal investigating team. In the 1969-data pilot study, for example, the units of analysis (the individual news stories) were assigned by the principal investigating team prior to showing the videotapes of the broadcasts to the coders. It is not a routine nor simple matter to identify the boundaries of a given story in all cases. Sometimes a second story which follows a first story is so similar in news content that it becomes difficult to decide whether one is dealing with two separate stories or rather with two aspects of the same story. In the pilot study, the principal investigators made such story assignments. In the 1972 study, the coders themselves were responsible for ascertaining the boundaries of the news stories, they were responsible for "unitizing" the entire news broadcasts.

In addition, the coding rules for the establishment of category applicability (the rules by which a story was placed in one category rather than in another) were much more precise in the 1972 study than in the 1969-data pilot study. The rationale in the pilot study was not to contaminate the sorting process of the coders by a too-rigid definition of category characteristics on the part of the principal investigators. One of the aims of the pilot project was to ascertain the extent to which coders would agree on the placement of stories given only a general set of category characteristic rules.

In the 1972 study, on the other hand, very precise definitions of categories were presented to the coders and very precise coding transformations were used in the coding of multiple categories (see Appendix A). Both techniques have an internal logic of their own, and both in themselves are valid intellectual attempts to get at the two-faced content-analytic problems of contamination and standardization. The fact that a number of similarities in, or at least complementing descriptions of, the various network news format and broadcasting styles for the 1969 data and the 1972 data is quite encouraging in that to some extent convergent validity is achieved for the applicability of both techniques.


### Description of the Coding Staff, 1972
### Campaign-Period News Coverage

Given the fact that both hard- and soft-content analytic techniques were used in this 1972 television news-content analysis and that unlike the pilot project a limited number of coders were recruited, it is necessary more closely to describe the personalities, media habits, and political preferences of the coders involved in the content-analytic operations of the 1972 project. A complete description of the recruiting techniques and training program is presented in Appendix A, the raw data from the initial questionnaires which all applicants filled out prior to acceptance into the coding team is presented in Appendix B,[18] and the differences in recruiting strategy between the 1969 and 1972 data were discussed above. Too often it is assumed that either the prior predispositions of the coders used in data generation is not of importance and has no effect upon the consequent coding of the given material, or that the prior predispositions are important but that the recruitment process will result in the selection of coders whose preferences and values are normally distributed across given key personality and behavioral dimensions.

In one sense, intercoder and intracoder reliabilities can offset the possible influences of coder bias, but while our reliability levels consistently held above 0.80, the possibility remains (as it does in any content analysis) that the error term was or is not randomly distributed. While techniques are being developed to locate the source and thus the directions of content-analytic unreliability or coder bias[19] and while efforts are underway to compensate for nonnormally distributed error in cited reliability formulas[20] at the present writing an optimal solution (and one which is presented below) is to describe closely those predispositions, preferences, and behavioral patterns of the coders who were involved in the crucial data generation aspect of the 1972 project. All following comments refer to those four coders who were used in the coding of the seven weeks of data from the fall of 1972.

Half of our coders received most national news from newspaper, the other half from television. Most had access regularly to a television, and evening-news viewing was evenly divided between the three networks and a "don't watch" response. Half of our coders considered themselves to be "regular viewers" of evening news programs. For the most part, our coders considered themselves to be magazine readers, and a series of questions which attempted to juxtapose magazines and radio as news sources with television revealed that former sources were quite often utilized. Thus our coding staff generally was a multimedia-using group.

Three of our four coders felt that network television news had not presented a fair picture of the domestic debate over the war in Southeast Asia, yet three of the four felt that protestors should not attempt to use the forum of the evening news to propagandize their own political positions. All agreed, however, that newscasters should be allowed to make editorial interpretations of the news, especially if those interpretations were thus labeled.

Our coding staff was quite interested in a wide range of issues and possible news topics, with the most interest being on the upcoming election, the Nixon administration, and the war in Southeast Asia (although not the Paris Peace Talks which might be indicative of a certain degree of cynicism and/or political sophistication, depending on one's own interpretation of the role of the Peace Talks in the resolution of the war). Interestingly enough, the least interest was shown in local (Philadelphia) politics, implying a certain greater receptivity and interest to national and international news than to local news.

As concerns their evaluations of the personalities who report the news, a series of semantic differential questions were presented in which the candidates for the recruiting staff were asked to rate the newscasters along a series of personality dimensions. John Chancellor seemed to get the most positive affecting rating followed by David Brinkley who was judged to be a little less interesting and a little more biased. Howard K. Smith produced the widest range of responses across the various categories, and both Walter Cronkite followed by Harry Reasoner were given the most "stable" (middle of the scales) scores.

We took three characteristics of news coverage—completeness, unbiased reporting, and accuracy—and constructed a three-item semantic differential scale by which the candidates were to rate the television news' coverage of specific issues. By assigning raw scores to each of the positions on the semantic differential scale and aggregating these scores across our four to-be-coders, we get some estimation of the coding staff's evaluation of the way in which the television news in general covered various news issues. The lower the aggregate score, the "better the job" the news media did in covering these issues. The results, taken from the raw data presented in Appendix B, are presented in Table 2-3.

Our coding staff felt the networks by far did the worst job of covering the Viet Cong, followed by their own coverage of the controversy that they (the news media) had become involved in. Our coders felt that the networks had done their best news coverage of the draft, the Nixon administration, and the Paris Peace Talks (although as stated above our coding staff was highly interested in the Nixon administration but not very interested in the Peace Talks).

While our coders were generally graduate students, the identification problems which they were asked to answer showed some degree of insulation from information and events of the political worlds around them. Half of our coding staff stated that they supported no major political party. These indications of apoliticality were somewhat important in the final selection of the coding staff.

Table 2-3

**Coding Staff Evaluations of Television News Coverage of Selected Political Issues: Clustered Semantic Differential Indices[a]**

| | |
|---|---|
| The draft | 2.75[b] |
| Nixon administration | 2.92 |
| Paris Peace Talks | 3.25 |
| Phase II Economic Policy | 3.50 |
| American election campaigns | 3.58 |
| War in Southeast Asia | 3.58 |
| Conflict in Northern Ireland | 3.67 |
| Prisoners of war | 4.00 |
| Ecology and pollution | 4.00 |
| Middle East Conflict | 4.17 |
| Racial conflicts | 4.17 |
| People's Republic of China | 4.50 |
| Military spending | 4.58 |
| Mass media | 4.67 |
| Students | 4.92 |
| The Viet Cong | 5.17 |

[a]1 = Complete, unbiased and accurate.
  7 = Incomplete, biased and inaccurate.
[b]Mean semantic differential scores for all coders.

In brief, we believe that we found a coding team characterized by a high degree of intelligence but of intelligence that for the most part was directed toward school and career interests. We were able to work with a broad range of general orientations toward a number of political issues and a broad spectrum of media use and media orientation. The coders, once selected and trained, were presented with a content-analytic protocol which created a series of data sets, these data sets to be described in the following section.

## Parallels in the Techniques and Findings of the 1969 and 1972 Data Studies

In the study of the network coverage of the 1972 presidential campaign, we opted for a greater emphasis upon "hard content analytic" procedures while retaining specific soft content analytic procedures developed in working with the 1969 data. Working within the general framework of network characteristics as discovered in our 1969 study, we attempt in the 1972 data and analysis which follows to present additional message characteristics too often overlooked by media analysts, message characteristics such as the visual components of the broadcast message.

In a very real sense, the findings of the 1969 study conducted by Cutler, Tedesco, and Frank were complemented by the findings of the 1972 campaign period. For example, those general stylistic characteristics which were identified by our coders in the 1969 study using holistic and somewhat soft-content analytic techniques were in large part "operationalized" and confirmed as operative in the 1972 study by looking at specific often-overlooked hard content analytic message characteristics.

The comparison of the data from the two complementary techniques can furthermore shed some interesting light upon specific coder-attribution rules that seem to be in operation across these two studies. For example, working with 1969 data, the coders cited CBS as the "most impartial" network. We shall show in the following section that in the 1972 data CBS has a strikingly larger number of "embarrassing stories" than does either ABC or NBC. Embarrassing stories can be attributed to a commitment to investigative journalism (and/or to more politically venal motives, the existence of which is neither asserted here nor important in the context of the present argument) which leads to "electronic exposés." The emphasis upon such investigative journalism might well lead to an image of impartiality in the eyes of the coders who view such a network style using soft-content analytic techniques, especially if the network does not avoid embarrassing one of the two major parties (as CBS did not hesitate to do, i.e., while the number of stories embarrassing to the Republicans was higher than on ABC and on NBC, the number embarrassing to the Democrats was approximately the same for all three networks).

Unfortunately, a complete comparison of hard and soft coding techniques and resulting evaluations of network news coverage cannot be drawn from the two studies now completed. A great number of interesting possibilities are available by comparing the results of the two general types of analysis, and the reader is invited to explore these results with an eye to comparative and inferential speculation. However, given the radically different nature of the news period being covered, a campaign versus a noncampaign period, given the major financial costs which would have had to be borne (which were not) to conduct soft as well as hard coding procedures on a sufficient quantity of news broadcasts, and given the fact that the sample sizes of the 1969 and 1972 studies are quite different, at best a series of interesting hypotheses can be generated by comparing the results of the 1969-data pilot study and the 1972 campaign-period study.

## Synopsis of Procedures Used in the 1972 Study

The data that follow are specifically drawn from the coding of the 1972 network news broadcasts. The twenty-nine message characteristics (twenty-five independent measures plus airtime duration, total number of story graphics, voice-over film, non-voice-over film, and filed reports) which were coded in the 1972 study are presented in summary form in Table 2-4. A more complete explanation of each variable and coder selection and training techniques may be found in in Appendix A.

## Table 2-4
## Summary Description of Variables Used in Message Analysis

*Story Identification Variables*:
Date identification
Network identification
Story placement
Commercial proximity
Editorial

*Visual and Durative Variables*:
Airtime allocation, story duration
Number and duration of story graphics
Number and duration of voice-over film segments
Number and duration of non-voice-over film segments
Number and duration of field reports
Type and duration of noncandidate interview of statement film segments

*Story-Type Variables*:
Issue identification, secondary issue identification
Hard news and soft news
Agency action

**Table 2-4 (cont.)**

---

*Vietnam Film Variables*:
Vietnam action visuals, secondary Vietnam action visuals
Vietnam: time attended dead or wound film segment; time covered dead;
time unattended dead

*Candidate Coverage*:
General candidate activity
Candidate association
Crowd coverage
Film time, candidate statement
Film time, candidate shown with voters
Tightshot coverage

*Commentary Variables*:
News commentary
Secondary news commentary

*Favorability Variables*:
Story content favorability
Story treatment favorability

---

Our analysis consists of coding of seven weeks of weeknight (Monday-Friday) television network news broadcasts during the 1972 campaign period. Every broadcast for all three major networks within the seven weeks was coded using 1/2" J-Format videotape facilities.[21] Data are therefore available and presented here in grouped form, for (1) an early campaign sample of the two weeks following the Democratic National Convention and the Republican National Convention, (2) a two-week midcampaign sample from September, and (3) a three-week closing-campaign sample beginning in mid-October and concluding with the network broadcasts on November 6, 1972.[22]

# 3

## Network News Coverage of the 1972 Presidential Election Campaign Period: A Review of the Data

### Introduction

Drawing upon the experiences of the pilot project and having developed techniques and recruited/trained our coding staff, we embarked upon a far more ambitious research program for examining seven weeks of national, weeknight, television evening newscasts. A total of thirty-five broadcasts per network were videotaped and coded, fifty-two-and-one-half hours of network news broadcasting in all. As described in Chapter 2, this sample included news broadcasts from the early, middle, and final stages of the 1972 campaign period.

In addition, we conducted parallel analyses of the *New York Times* for the same days as the evening news broadcasts. Principles of data comparison and results of this coding effort are presented later in this section. Comparisons will be made between print and electronic journalism for the sample period involved. Finally, a somewhat exploratory comparison was made between network news coverage and public responses as reported in nationally-administered survey research reports from this same campaign period. We are working here with secondary data sources and all results are somewhat tentative. Nevertheless, trends in network news coverage and trends in perceived salience of various political issues are presented in the latter section of Chapter 3.

### Review of the Network News Broadcasts

Table 3-1 presents airtime duration and story-placement data for these three groups of broadcasts. Airtime duration is measured as a percentage of the total airtime devoted for news, by network, for the given broadcast weeks. Story placement scores represent mean placement for the given category across the broadcast weeks, the story placement scores here expressed as relative placements after number of stories in the sample groups are controlled.[1] The data presented in Table 3-1 represent story inclusion in a category as either a "primary" or as a "secondary" issue. (Coders were allowed to code each story into a maximum of two issue categories.) The mean reliability score associated with primary and secondary coding technique was 0.82 using the Holsti reliability formula.[2] Further "grouping" of the forty-six issue categories used would probably further increase this reliability score. In the case of rank-ordering of "Top 3" non-Vietnam foreign stories and the "Top 5" nonparty domestic stories, "foreign, other" and "domestic, other" stories are omitted

37

**Table 3-1**
**Grouped and Aggregate Airtime Duration and Relative Story Placement**

### ABC July-August

| | % | $\bar{X}_{rp}$ [c] |
|---|---|---|
| Vietnam | 10.8 | .45 |
| Foreign | 31.2 | .49 |
| Domestic | 68.8 | .49 |
| Top 3 %-stories, Vietnam | | |
| Military | 6.4 | .44 |
| Politics | 2.0 | .38 |
| Air war | 1.5 | .46 |
| Top 3 %-stories, foreign non-Vtnm | | |
| Asia, NVM [a] | 5.5 | .34 |
| Mideast | 3.8 | .51 |
| Ireland | 3.2 | .54 |
| Party coverage | | |
| Democrat | 20.0 | .31 |
| Republn' | 7.3 | .41 |
| Top 5 %-stories, domestic | | |
| Finance | 8.2 | .35 |
| Labor | 6.0 | .18 |
| Crime | 5.0 | .75 |
| Ecology | 3.3 | .68 |
| Mil. aff. | 1.8 | .45 |

### ABC September

| | % | $\bar{X}_{rp}$ |
|---|---|---|
| Vietnam | 10.8 | .34 |
| Foreign | 26.6 | .48 |
| Domestic | 73.4 | .52 |
| Top 3 %-stories, Vietnam | | |
| Military | 2.9 | .27 |
| Air war | 2.8 | .31 |
| POW's | 2.0 | .45 |

### CBS July-August

| | % | $\bar{X}_{rp}$ |
|---|---|---|
| Vietnam | 12.1 | .38 |
| Foreign | 23.7 | .43 |
| Domestic | 76.3 | .51 |
| Military | 5.4 | .43 |
| Politics | 2.4 | .26 |
| Other | 1.5 | .27 |
| Mideast | 2.5 | .37 |
| Ireland | 2.5 | .59 |
| Eur-NNATO [b] | 1.8 | .88 |
| Democrat | 19.7 | .33 |
| Republn' | 13.5 | .35 |
| Crime | 5.5 | .72 |
| Labor | 5.4 | .25 |
| Finance | 5.4 | .56 |
| Ecology | 3.5 | .82 |
| Ethics | 2.6 | .47 |

### CBS September

| | % | $\bar{X}_{rp}$ |
|---|---|---|
| Vietnam | 17.8 | .32 |
| Foreign | 36.8 | .41 |
| Domestic | 63.2 | .57 |
| Air war | 5.0 | .29 |
| Military | 3.6 | .27 |
| Politics | 2.8 | .51 |

### NBC July-August

| | % | $\bar{X}_{rp}$ |
|---|---|---|
| Vietnam | 17.2 | .30 |
| Foreign | 30.8 | .43 |
| Domestic | 69.2 | .55 |
| Air war | 7.1 | .26 |
| Military | 4.7 | .25 |
| Politics | 4.0 | .25 |
| Asia, NVM | 3.9 | .31 |
| Mideast | 2.6 | .47 |
| Ireland | 1.0 | .54 |
| Democrat | 14.7 | .33 |
| Republn' | 10.8 | .39 |
| Labor | 7.1 | .36 |
| Finance | 4.5 | .70 |
| Ethics | 4.0 | .49 |
| Crime | 3.2 | .75 |
| Ecology | 2.2 | .65 |

### NBC September

| | % | $\bar{X}_{rp}$ |
|---|---|---|
| Vietnam | 20.4 | .34 |
| Foreign | 37.0 | .45 |
| Domestic | 63.0 | .51 |
| Air war | 5.4 | .36 |
| Military | 5.1 | .28 |
| Other | 3.4 | .46 |

## ABC / CBS / NBC — October

| | ABC October | | | | | | NBC October | | |
|---|---|---|---|---|---|---|---|---|---|
| **Top 3 %-stories, foreign non-Vtnm** | Mideast | 5.8 | .54 | Mideast | 6.1 | .47 | Mideast | 5.3 | .48 |
| | Africa | 3.8 | .67 | Africa | 3.4 | .42 | Sov-West | 2.7 | .45 |
| | Eur-NNATO | 1.7 | .56 | Eur-NNATO | 2.7 | .58 | Asia, NVM | 1.8 | .81 |
| **Party coverage** | Democrat | 19.2 | .38 | Democrat | 14.4 | .37 | Democrat | 14.9 | .36 |
| | Republn' | 18.0 | .39 | Republn' | 15.3 | .46 | Republn' | 13.5 | .30 |
| **Top 5 %-stories, domestic** | Finance | 4.6 | .74 | Crime | 5.5 | .55 | Crime | 4.1 | .69 |
| | Ethics | 4.4 | .35 | Ethics | 5.4 | .42 | Ethics | 2.7 | .37 |
| | Farms | 4.4 | .33 | Finance | 2.5 | .71 | Ecology | 2.6 | .76 |
| | Consumers | 2.3 | .76 | Farms | 2.3 | .41 | Mil. aff. | 2.3 | .58 |
| | Urban aff | 2.2 | .87 | Wg-prc | 1.9 | .71 | Finance | 2.2 | .70 |

| | CBS October | | | | | | | | |
|---|---|---|---|---|---|---|---|---|---|
| **Top 3 %-stories, Vietnam** | Vietnam | 26.5 | .30 | Vietnam | 22.2 | .29 | Vietnam | 27.1 | .30 |
| | Foreign | 33.9 | .43 | Foreign | 28.9 | .43 | Foreign | 37.8 | .42 |
| | Domestic | 66.1 | .58 | Domestic | 71.1 | .60 | Domestic | 62.2 | .55 |
| | Politics | 16.1 | .26 | Politics | 10.6 | .22 | Politics | 18.7 | .29 |
| | Military | 6.2 | .31 | Other | 4.8 | .61 | Military | 5.0 | .28 |
| | Other | 1.8 | .42 | Military | 4.2 | .30 | POW's | 1.3 | .46 |
| **Top 3 %-stories, foreign non-Vtnm** | Eur-NNATO | 2.0 | .82 | Eur-NNATO | 1.2 | .80 | Eur-NNATO | 2.9 | .86 |
| | Mideast | 1.5 | .86 | Mideast | 1.0 | .76 | Sov-West | 1.4 | .66 |
| | Asia, Vmr[d] | 0.7 | .81 | Latin Amer | 0.8 | .76 | Mideast | 1.2 | .58 |
| **Party coverage** | Democrat | 17.6 | .49 | Democrat | 16.7 | .57 | Democrat | 16.5 | .45 |
| | Republn' | 24.4 | .51 | Republn' | 26.6 | .57 | Republn' | 19.0 | .45 |
| **Top 5 %-stories, domestic** | Ethics | 5.1 | .48 | Ethics | 7.4 | .50 | Ethics | 3.3 | .41 |
| | Finance | 3.2 | .68 | Civil rt. | 3.1 | .62 | Finance | 3.1 | .73 |
| | Civil rt | 2.9 | .82 | Finance | 3.1 | .71 | Crime | 2.5 | .63 |
| | Crime | 2.1 | .77 | HEW | 2.8 | .48 | Mil. aff. | 1.5 | .51 |
| | HEW | 1.4 | .61 | Crime | 2.0 | .64 | Civil rt. | 1.4 | .72 |

**Table 3-1** (cont.)

Total Aggregated Data Across Entire Seven-Week Sample

| | ABC | | | CBS | | | NBC | | |
|---|---|---|---|---|---|---|---|---|---|
| | Vietnam | 17.6 | .33 | Vietnam | 18.3 | .32 | Vietnam | 22.3 | .31 |
| | Foreign | 30.9 | .46 | Foreign | 29.6 | .42 | Foreign | 35.6 | .44 |
| | Domestic | 69.1 | .54 | Domestic | 70.4 | .56 | Domestic | 64.4 | .54 |
| Top 3 %-stories, Vietnam | Politics | 7.5 | .27 | Politics | 6.3 | .27 | Politics | 9.4 | .29 |
| | Military | 5.2 | .34 | Military | 4.4 | .34 | Military | 4.9 | .27 |
| | Air war | 1.8 | .31 | Other | 3.1 | .44 | Air war | 3.9 | .31 |
| Top 3 %-stories, foreign non-Vtnm | Mideast | 3.4 | .61 | Mideast | 2.8 | .55 | Mideast | 2.8 | .50 |
| | Eur-NNATO | 1.8 | .75 | Eur-NNATO | 1.8 | .72 | Asia, NVM | 1.9 | .61 |
| | Asia, NVM | 1.7 | .44 | Sov-West | 1.0 | .53 | Eur-NNATO | 1.7 | .69 |
| Party coverage | Democrat | 18.7 | .40 | Democrat | 16.9 | .44 | Democrat | 15.5 | .39 |
| | Republn' | 17.9 | .47 | Republn' | 20.0 | .49 | Republn' | 15.1 | .40 |
| Top 5 %-stories, domestic | Finance | 4.9 | .61 | Ethics | 5.5 | .47 | Ethics | 3.3 | .42 |
| | Ethics | 3.6 | .42 | Crime | 3.9 | .64 | Finance | 3.2 | .71 |
| | Crime | 2.8 | .73 | Finance | 3.6 | .66 | Crime | 3.2 | .68 |
| | Labor | 2.1 | .36 | Civil rt. | 2.0 | .65 | Labor | 2.6 | .47 |
| | Civil rt | 1.5 | .76 | Mil aff. | 1.9 | .60 | Ecology | 1.7 | .70 |

[a] Asia, non-Vietnam related.
[b] European affairs, non-NATO related.
[c] $\bar{X}_{rp}$ is the mean relative placement score.
[d] + Asian story, Vietnam related.

from possible rank-order positions since these are residual categories and include relatively minor issues.

Amount of airtime given to specific stories and story-types certainly has an impact upon the perceived importance (and perhaps the credibility[3]) of a given news story. Voluminous research has also shown the importance of the serial order of presentation as a factor influencing credibility and story-retention,[4] although most of this work has been done using either oral or written arguments. The impact of serial order of presentation may be different when the message is communicated via radio and/or television.[5] Especially in the case of television, further research has been called for in studying this aspect of the television news broadcast.[6]

Table 3-1 shows that among network news broadcasts for our 1972 election period sample such differences in airtime duration and serial order of presentation do exist. NBC devoted almost twice as much airtime across the seven weeks to Vietnam as did ABC. On all three networks, Vietnam stories generally were presented "high" (earlier) on the story-board format. CBS devoted more airtime to "Government Ethics" stories than did NBC or ABC, yet these two networks had a higher mean story placement than did CBS for this category of news stories.

There are a series of other characteristics of the news message, however, which we feel are equally, if not more, important than simple airtime-duration and story-placement measures. A few of these dimensions will be explained and discussed here.

One of the measures on which we collected data was "agency action." Regardless of the explicit "content" of the news story, we ascertained whether or not an "agency" was portrayed as acting in the given news story. For example, a story concerning "civil rights" may have dealt with a Supreme Court decision. Thus, while the "issue" was coded as civil rights, the "agency action" dimension was scored for "Supreme Court."

Our results from "agency action" scoring are startling. While September was generally a "legislative action" sample and October a "judicial action" sample, the overwhelming emphasis across all three networks was in covering "executive action" to the exclusion of judicial and legislative action. These data are presented in Table 3-2.

To the best of our knowledge, no major study of television news has concerned itself with this dimension. Yet a series of crucial questions are raised by the data presented in Table 3-2. Given the fact that for our seven-week sample "executive action" stories outnumbered "legislative action" and "judicial action" combined, what effect does this have upon audiences in terms of prescribed and/or effectively portrayed political action? Can it be argued that such reporting communicates to politically active audiences the message that they should look to executive organs of government in order to realize satisfaction for political, social, and economic needs and desires? In terms of the

**Table 3-2**

**Agency-Action Data, Grouped and Aggregate, by Network**

| | July-August | | | September | | |
|---|---|---|---|---|---|---|
| | ABC | CBS | NBC | ABC | CBS | NBC |
| Supreme Court | 1[a] | 1 | 1 | 0 | 0 | 1 |
| Congress, general | 0 | 1 | 0 | 0 | 0 | 1 |
| Senate | 4 | 3 | 4 | 9 | 9 | 13 |
| House | 2 | 5 | 2 | 4 | 3 | 2 |
| Executive | 7 | 9 | 11 | 6 | 12 | 16 |
| Lower court | 1 | 2 | 4 | 4 | 7 | 7 |
| Agency | 11 | 13 | 14 | 5 | 6 | 5 |
| State executive | 1 | 1 | 0 | 0 | 1 | 1 |
| Local government | 0 | 3 | 1 | 3 | 0 | 4 |
| Judicial | 2 | 3 | 5 | 4 | 8 | 8 |
| Legislative | 6 | 9 | 6 | 13 | 13 | 16 |
| Executive | 19 | 26 | 26 | 14 | 19 | 26 |
| | October | | | Across 7 Weeks | | |
| | ABC | CBS | NBC | ABC | CBS | NBC |
| Supreme Court | 5 | 3 | 5 | 6 | 5 | 7 |
| Congress, general | 3 | 3 | 3 | 3 | 5 | 5 |
| Senate | 1 | 1 | 0 | 14 | 13 | 17 |
| House | 1 | 1 | 1 | 7 | 9 | 5 |
| Executive | 15 | 10 | 18 | 28 | 31 | 45 |
| Lower court | 5 | 5 | 4 | 10 | 14 | 15 |
| Agency | 4 | 2 | 3 | 20 | 21 | 22 |
| State executive | 0 | 2 | 2 | 1 | 4 | 3 |
| Local government | 2 | 0 | 1 | 5 | 3 | 7 |
| Judicial | 10 | 8 | 9 | 16 | 19 | 22 |
| Legislative | 5 | 5 | 4 | 24 | 27 | 27 |
| Executive | 21 | 14 | 24 | 54 | 49 | 75 |

[a]Represents number of stories with given category of action.

1972 elections in which a senator (legislative) and an incumbent president were matched in a race for the presidency, does it make a difference that during the crucial last three weeks of the election between three and six times as many stories included messages of "executive" as opposed to "legislative" action? It has been suggested that one of the most important benefits of cable television will be to allow audiences to become familiar with and realize the action possibilities of local legislative and quasi-administrative organs of government.[7] If this is indeed the case, then we must consider the possibility that such an "unbalanced" presentation of agency action at the national level which is communicated by network news does have an important effect upon mass orientation toward the political process.[8]

We find differences not only in the oral (or textual) messages broadcast by the network evening news but also in the *visual film themes and techniques of filming* used in portraying both candidates and issues. The importance of film technique in affecting the vividness of power of a given film is well documented by film theorists and critics.[9] Through the use of different strategies of filming, for example, a candidate can be projected as either warm, loved, and intimate or as cold, perhaps feared,[10] and distant. Through the use of "tightshots," that is, film shot from close to the individual in which only a part of his body (generally his face) is captured on film, the former image can be projected. Film in which the candidate is shown at a distance may tend to the latter effect. The amount of film showing a candidate mixing with and meeting voters (and being well received), is a measure of broadcasted warmth and lovableness.

In addition, the *type* of film used, either "voice-over" or "non-voice-over" film, has an impact on the projected image or issue. It is generally agreed that voice-over film (film with a narrator's voice accompanying the visual message) is less stark, less "real," and less "on the spot" than non-voice-over newsfilm, the latter being greatly similar to the *cinema verite* technique used in documentaries and in some movies.

The use of film is itself a variable which must be taken into account, especially in the coverage of controversial news items. Furthermore, the vividness of what is shown may vary irrespectively of the verbal content of the news report. For example, the airtime duration of film showing dead bodies or wounded personnel during network Vietnam coverage may be an important, if relatively infrequent, film theme.

For the seven weeks of our 1972 sample, we have coded all these dimensions of the television news message. Table 3-3 presents grouped and aggregate data from our "tightshots" coverage. A "mean" tightshots score for each candidate, by network, is presented. Note, however, that this "mean" score is not a true mean since at this stage of our research we cannot be certain that the eight categories of tightshot scoring represent interval categories. However, as an exploratory mean, the data in Table 3-3 presents some startling results.

Across the seven-week sample, the number of stories in which film of McGovern is used is approximately equal to the total number of stories using film for Nixon, Agnew, and Shriver. McGovern, moreover, is presented as the most intimate (highest mean tightshot score) of the four candidates.

Moreover, there are different levels of "tight-shot advantage" for McGovern over Nixon in the grouped data. Using the exploratory means we have generated, it is apparent that September was Nixon's "best sample" in terms of tightshot coverage and October (the month that Nixon was publically campaigning more often) was the most disadvantageous to the president on this dimension. Only on

**Table 3-3**

**Grouped and Aggregate Data, Tightshot Scoring, by Network and Candidate**

| | July-August Sample | | | | September Sample | | |
|---|---|---|---|---|---|---|---|
| | ABC | CBS | NBC | | ABC | CBS | NBC |
| McGovern | 4.71[a] | 5.44 | 5.44 | McGovern | 4.12 | 6.12 | 5.55 |
| Shriver | 3.00 | 0 | 0 | Shriver | 0 | 0 | 4.00 |
| Nixon | 3.00 | 2.66 | 2.75 | Nixon | 4.00 | 3.75 | 5.50 |
| Agnew | 0 | 0 | 0 | Agnew | 4.00 | 4.50 | 4.66 |
| Eagleton | 5.00 | 5.00 | 7.00 | | | | |

| | October Sample | | | | Seven-week Aggregate Sample | | |
|---|---|---|---|---|---|---|---|
| | ABC | CBS | NBC | | ABC | CBS | NBC |
| McGovern | 5.46 | 5.56 | 5.31 | McGovern | 4.89 | 5.54 | 5.41 |
| Shriver | 5.00 | 3.00 | 5.25 | Shriver | 4.50 | 3.00 | 4.71 |
| Nixon | 2.67 | 4.20 | 2.17 | Nixon | 2.93 | 3.82 | 2.92 |
| Agnew | 4.17 | 4.00 | 5.20 | Agnew | 4.11 | 4.12 | 4.44 |
| | | | | Eagleton | 5.00 | 5.00 | 7.00 |

[a]Represents "heuristic mean" score on an eight-point scale, "1" equals "most distant" tightshot and "8" equals closest camera shot possible with weighting for camera angle. Categories are assumed to be at least ordinal, with the higher the mean representing the more intimate and close the tightshot.

CBS did Nixon's tightshot scoring relative to McGovern's improve from September to October.

McGovern also enjoyed an airtime duration over Nixon in terms of film showing him speaking and film showing him mixing with the people. Again it is of interest that across the seven-week sample, with the exception of CBS, Agnew was shown on more film making political statements than was his presidential running mate, Nixon, although this might be expected since the president did less personal campaigning. Chester has shown that simple appearance on television cannot predict electoral success,[11] and it can be argued that lack of airtime film (perhaps consciously avoided) might have facilitated the authority and busy-responsible image that Nixon was apparently attempting to portray. Often candidates themselves will attempt to structure even these film dimensions of television coverage of their activities.[12]

Dimensions of candidate news coverage such as time-with-voters and tightshot coverage do show differences both across time and to some extent across networks in our seven-week campaign-period sample.

Table 3-4 presents a complementary film dimension to Table 3-3's tightshot coverage. Table 3-4, without controlling for the degree of tightshot coverage, presents the film time for the candidates' "mixing with voters" and their "time on film speaking." Again the Nixon data are really too limited to make any valid

**Table 3-4**
**Grouped and Aggregate Data, Film Time for Statements and Time with Voters by Candidate, by Network Coverage**

| | July-August | | | | September | | |
|---|---|---|---|---|---|---|---|
| | Time on Film Speaking | | | | Time on Film Speaking | | |
| | ABC | CBS | NBC | | ABC | CBS | NBC |
| McGovern | 317[a] | 548 | 375 | McGovern | 321 | 314 | 412 |
| Shriver | 00 | 00 | 00 | Shriver | 00 | 00 | 52 |
| Nixon | 00 | 00 | 35 | Nixon | 94 | 140 | 90 |
| Agnew | 00 | 00 | 00 | Agnew | 98 | 8 | 208 |
| | Time with Voters, Film | | | | Time with Voters, Film | | |
| | ABC | CBS | NBC | | ABC | CBS | NBC |
| McGovern | 109 | 195 | 167 | McGovern | 179 | 234 | 228 |
| Shriver | 00 | 00 | 00 | Shriver | 00 | 00 | 63 |
| Nixon | 122 | 69 | 64 | Nixon | 31 | 15 | 37 |
| Agnew | 00 | 00 | 00 | Agnew | 8 | 00 | 39 |
| | October | | | | Totals | | |
| | Time on Film Speaking | | | | Time of Film Speaking | | |
| | ABC | CBS | NBC | | ABC | CBS | NBC |
| McGovern | 928 | 718 | 524 | McGovern | 1566 | 1580 | 1311 |
| Shriver | 92 | 20 | 153 | Shriver | 92 | 20 | 205 |
| Nixon | 265 | 418 | 185 | Nixon | 359 | 558 | 310 |
| Agnew | 306 | 235 | 208 | Agnew | 404 | 375 | 416 |
| | Time with Voters, Film | | | | Time with Voters, Film | | |
| | ABC | CBS | NBC | | ABC | CBS | NBC |
| McGovern | 184 | 397 | 232 | McGovern | 472 | 826 | 627 |
| Shriver | 105 | 16 | 91 | Shriver | 105 | 16 | 154 |
| Nixon | 146 | 275 | 130 | Nixon | 299 | 359 | 231 |
| Agnew | 17 | 40 | 13 | Agnew | 25 | 40 | 52 |

[a]Total seconds of film time.

Nixon-McGovern comparisons on this dimension. Nevertheless, the breakdowns in Table 3-5 are quite revealing in terms of a Shriver-Agnew comparison.

Across the seven-week sample period and aggregating across networks, Shriver is shown "mixing with the people" much more than is Agnew, while the vice-president is given more airtime coverage during which he is making political statements. Again, different "film images" are generated: Shriver, the man of the people, who is loved by, and loves the crowds; and Agnew, the man of authority,

**Table 3-5**

Aggregate Data, Selected News Topics, Voice-Over and Non-Voice-Over Data, by Network

| | ABC | | | CBS | | | NBC | | |
|---|---|---|---|---|---|---|---|---|---|
| | VO[a] | NVO[b] | NVO/VO | VO | NVO | NVO/VO | VO | NVO | NVO/VO |
| Air war | 401[c] | 180 | .45 | 303 | 463 | 1.53 | 1438 | 439 | .30 |
| All Vietnam stories | 3659 | 1757 | .48 | 3921 | 3392 | .86 | 5675 | 2327 | .41 |
| Democratic party | 3607 | 4167 | 1.16 | 4237 | 3778 | .89 | 3147 | 3475 | 1.10 |
| Republican party | 3355 | 3636 | 1.08 | 4924 | 3401 | .69 | 3122 | 2444 | .78 |

[a]Voice-over.
[b]Non-voice over.
[c]Total number of seconds.

who takes a political stand, who speaks from the feeling of internal conviction predicated upon his ability and experience in making political decisions. Whether these personal characteristics indeed hold true or not, differential film coverage tends to portray such different personality images.

Table 3-5 presents data from some selected categories which show, across the seven-week sample, differential use of voice-over and non-voice-over film by the three national networks. If the film theorists are correct in arguing that non-voice-over film is more immediate, memorable, and real, the Democrats enjoyed an advantage on this dimension across the seven-week sample.

With the exception of CBS, Table 3-5 also shows an interesting distinction between Democratic and Republican party coverage, the most thoroughly covered domestic categories, and Vietnam war coverage, the most thoroughly covered foreign news category. On ABC and NBC, as the news coverage switches from domestic American politics to news from the Vietnam war, the proportion of the non-voice-over to voice-over film drops by over 50 percent, that is, the relative use of vivid and immediate non-voice-over film decreases significantly. During our seven-week sample the American political process is brought into the American living room by NBC and ABC with a sense of reality and immediacy which is not equalled by these networks' coverage of the war in Vietnam.

We also see a similarity between ABC and NBC on another film dimension concerning stories on the Vietnam war. We coded film themes of footage broadcasted during stories dealing with the war. The film themes do not necessarily correspond with the major emphasis of the given story. For example, a story dealing with ARVN-attempts to rout the Viet Cong may highlight the use of air power in the film that accompanies the story, either by showing results of previous saturation bombing or by showing fighter bombers or helicopter gunships engaged in tactical air strikes. In this case, a story that would ordinarily be coded as "Vietnam, ground 'military' action" may be coded in terms of film as "Results of Air War."

Table 3-6 shows the results of primary and secondary coding, or first and second film themes, from all stories in which war-zone footage was broadcast over the evening news. Like the general categories of issue identification, coders were allowed to code all the film for a given Vietnam war story in one or two categories. One category was used if the film had only one theme, that is, portrayed only one of the categories of our Vietnam "action film" coding protocol. If two or more themes were portrayed in the film associated with a given story, a second film-theme category was scored. The grouped and aggregate data for the Vietnam action visuals are presented.

Looking at the total number of film segments across the seven weeks of our sample, it is clear that NBC has the greatest number of different film segments. Using the "heuristic mean" technique described above, we can see that NBC, followed by ABC, presented the "bloodiest" Vietnam war footage. CBS, although it gave more airtime to the Vietnam war than did ABC, presents a

**Table 3-6**
**Vietnam Visuals, Film Themes, Grouped Data**

| July-August | ABC | CBS | NBC |
|---|---|---|---|
| (1) People living, no violence | 1[a] (1-0)[b] | 0 (0-0) | 3 (2-1) |
| (2) Battle scene, shows desolation | 0 (0-0) | 0 (0-0) | 0 (0-0) |
| (3) Soldiers in operation, no enemy contact | 1 (1-0) | 3 (3-0) | 3 (3-0) |
| (4) Soldiers in operation, enemy contact | 3 (3-0) | 0 (0-0) | 3 (1-2) |
| (5) Wounded soldiers | 1 (1-0) | 1 (1-0) | 2 (1-1) |
| (6) Results of air war | 3 (1-2) | 1 (0-1) | 8 (4-4) |
| (7) Casualties | 1 (0-1) | 0 (0-0) | 1 (0-1) |
| (8) Results of N. Vietnam terror | 0 (0-0) | 0 (0-0) | 0 (0-0) |
| (9) Wounded, maimed or infirm civilian personnel | 0 (0-0) | 0 (0-0) | 3 (3-0) |
| | N = 10, 7-3 | N = 5, 4-1 | N = 23, 14-9 |
| | $\overline{X}$ = 4.60[c] | $\overline{X}$ = 4.00 | $\overline{X}$ = 3.87 |

| September | | | |
|---|---|---|---|
| (1) People living, no violence | 1 (1-0) | 1 (1-0) | 3 (2-1) |
| (2) Battle scene, shows desolation | 2 (1-1) | 2 (2-0) | 3 (2-1) |
| (3) Soldiers in operation, no enemy contact | 3 (2-1) | 2 (0-2) | 2 (1-1) |
| (4) Soldiers in operation, enemy contact | 1 (1-0) | 1 (1-0) | 1 (1-0) |
| (5) Wounded soldiers | 0 (0-0) | 0 (0-0) | 0 (0-0) |
| (6) Results of air war | 0 (0-0) | 1 (1-0) | 4 (2-2) |
| (7) Casualties | 0 (0-0) | 0 (0-0) | 1 (0-1) |
| (8) Results of N. Vietnam terror | 0 (0-0) | 0 (0-0) | 0 (0-0) |
| (9) Wounded, maimed, or infirm civilian personnel | 1 (0-1) | 0 (0-0) | 0 (0-0) |
| | N = 8, 5-3 | N = 7, 5-2 | N = 14, 8-6 |
| | $\overline{X}$ = 3.38 | $\overline{X}$ = 3.00 | $\overline{X}$ = 3.57 |

| October | | | |
|---|---|---|---|
| (1) People living, no violence | 5 (4-1) | 5 (2-3) | 8 (7-1) |
| (2) Battle scene, shows desolation | 1 (1-0) | 1 (1-0) | 1 (1-0) |
| (3) Soldiers in operation, no enemy contact | 3 (3-0) | 1 (1-0) | 3 (2-1) |
| (4) Soldiers in operation, enemy contact | 1 (1-0) | 3 (3-0) | 4 (3-1) |
| (5) Wounded soldiers | 1 (1-0) | 4 (1-3) | 2 (1-1) |
| (6) Results of air war | 0 (0-0) | 1 (1-0) | 0 (0-0) |
| (7) Casualties | 2 (0-2) | 0 (0-0) | 0 (0-0) |
| (8) Results of N. Vietnam terror | 1 (1-0) | 0 (0-0) | 0 (0-0) |
| (9) Wounded, maimed, or infirm civilian personnel | 0 (0-0) | 0 (0-0) | 0 (0-0) |
| | N = 14, 11-3 | N = 15, 9-6 | N = 18, 13-4 |
| | $\overline{X}$ = 3.36 | $\overline{X}$ = 3.20 | $\overline{X}$ = 2.50 |

**Table 3-6** (cont.)

| | Totals ABC | CBS | NBC |
|---|---|---|---|
| (1) People living, no violence | 7 (6-1) | 6 (3-3) | 14 (11-3) |
| (2) Battle scene, shows desolation | 3 (2-1) | 3 (3-0) | 4 (3-1) |
| (3) Soldiers in operation, no enemy contact | 7 (6-1) | 6 (4-2) | 8 (6-2) |
| (4) Soldiers in operation, enemy contact | 5 (5-0) | 4 (4-0) | 8 (5-3) |
| (5) Wounded soldiers | 2 (2-0) | 5 (2-3) | 4 (2-2) |
| (6) Results of air war | 3 (1-2) | 3 (2-1) | 12 (6-6) |
| (7) Casualties | 3 (0-3) | 0 (0-0) | 0 (0-0) |
| (8) Results of N. Vietnam terror | 1 (1-0) | 0 (0-0) | 0 (0-0) |
| (9) Wounded, maimed, or infirm personnel | 1 (0-1) | 0 (0-0) | 3 (3-0) |
| | N = 32, 23-9 | N = 27, 18-9 | N = 55, 36-19 |
| | $\overline{X}$ = 3.75 | $\overline{X}$ = 3.48 | $\overline{X}$ = 3.87 |

aTotal number of stories in which given category theme appears.

bContributions to total from first, followed by second, Vietnam action visuals coding.

cMean generated from total cases assuming ordinal categories and "heuristic mean" characteristics.

somewhat more "sanitized" and nonbloody picture of the war in terms of film footage eventually broadcast although CBS used the greatest proportion of non-voice-over to voice-over film. NBC presented the greatest number of total film themes, and the most bloody footage of all three networks, but also used the least amount of non-voice-over film.

ABC and NBC also lead CBS in terms of what we have called the "television body count." The number of seconds during which the evening news used film showing (1) "attended" dead and/or wounded (collapsed into one category when it became clear that in some cases fatalities and casualties could not be distinguished on film), (2) "covered" dead (film shots of bodies covered by ponchos, blankets, or generally being processed), and "unattended" dead (bodies lying uncared for in ditches, beside roads, etc.). The seven-week totals are presented in Table 3-7.

Table 3-7 shows that ABC led NBC and CBS in number of seconds with film showing attended dead and wounded with NBC running second. NBC led ABC and CBS with the greatest amount of covered and unattended dead body footage, with ABC running second. Thus, through use of an index independent of Vietnam-action visual themes we get roughly the same results, thus providing external validation to the scoring protocols used here.

We also scored story favorability and treatment favorability on a liberal-conservative scale for every story on all networks during the seven-week sample. (For a full explanation of liberal and conservative, see Appendix A.) The process used was semantic differential scaling. The reader is referred to Osgood's classic study of semantic meaning for an introduction to the use of this technique.[13]

Table 3-7

Aggregate Data, "Television Body Count" Airtime Duration for Vietnam War Footage, by Network

|  | ABC | CBS | NBC |
|---|---|---|---|
| Attended dead and/or wounded | 225[a] | 49 | 109 |
| Covered dead | 2 | 0 | 0 |
| Unattended dead | 7 | 0 | 15 |

[a]Represents seconds of airtime.

We found that taking all stories across the seven-week sample there was only a slight liberal favorability and only slightly more favorable story treatment toward the liberal end of the semantic differential scale.[14] There was very little change across the three grouped sample weeks, with the liberal position only slightly more favored during September sample weeks. NBC's October story favorability was the only score to present the conservatives in more favorable light than the liberals, while CBS was generally scored by our coders as presenting stories slightly more favorable to the liberals than NBC and ABC. These data are presented in Table 3-8.

When we selected only those stories dealing with George McGovern and Richard Nixon, a slightly different picture appeared. While story favorability went in the predicted direction (closer to "7," the liberal end of the semantic differential scale, for McGovern and closer to "1," the conservative end of the semantic differential scale, for Nixon), story *treatment* scores did not follow the same pattern. Looking at the seven-week sample, story treatment of the McGovern stories was not as favorable to the liberal position as were the objective parameters (tightshots, candidate film time, etc.) of the stories themselves. Likewise, networks' treatment of the Nixon stories was markedly less favorable to Nixon than the content of the stories themselves. For ABC and

Table 3-8

Semantic Differential Scoring, All Stories, Grouped and Aggregate Data

|  | July-August | | |  | September | | |
|---|---|---|---|---|---|---|---|
|  | ABC | CBS | NBC |  | ABC | CBS | NBC |
| Story treatment | 4.10[a] | 4.14 | 4.15 | Story treatment | 4.12 | 4.21 | 4.06 |
| Story favorability | 4.03 | 4.14 | 4.17 | Story favorability | 4.15 | 4.29 | 4.13 |
|  | October | | |  | Totals | | |
|  | ABC | CBS | NBC |  | ABC | CBS | NBC |
| Story treatment | 4.07 | 4.12 | 4.05 | Story treatment | 4.09 | 4.16 | 4.07 |
| Story favorability | 4.02 | 4.09 | 3.92 | Story favorability | 4.06 | 4.16 | 4.07 |

[a]Represents mean score on a "1" to "7" scale where the value of the midpoint is "4.00." "1" equals most favorable to conservatives, "7" equals most favorable to liberals.

CBS, stories dealing with Nixon actually were more favorable to the liberal than to the conservative position, a finding without comparison in McGovern story coverage. We found that story favorability and treatment favorability could, and should, be kept analytically distinct. A story might deal with Nixon's attempts to win the blue-collar vote, with story favorability probably being coded between "1" and "3" (the conservative end) on the semantic differential scale. Yet, it might also include a long statement by a labor leader saying that he would never vote for a president who initiated wage and price controls without putting a similar damper on profits and interest. As such, the "treatment of the story" (i.e., showing the labor leader's statement) would be favorable to the liberals, and would be coded on a supplementary dimension as perhaps a "5" to a "7" (the liberal end of the semantic differential scale). The semantic differential scoring for McGovern and Nixon stories is presented in Table 3-9.

In analyzing the story favorability data, the most important thing to note is the distance of the scores from neutral 4. In every case in Table 3-9,

**Table 3-9**
**Semantic Differential Scoring for McGovern and Nixon Stories, Grouped and Aggregate Data**

| McGovern | July-August | | | September | | | |
|---|---|---|---|---|---|---|---|
| | ABC | CBS | NBC | McGovern | ABC | CBS | NBC |
| Story treatment | 4.57[a] | 4.44 | 4.00 | Story treatment | 4.62 | 5.00 | 4.11 |
| Story favorability | 5.00 | 5.00 | 5.11 | Story favorability | 5.25 | 6.25 | 5.44 |
| Distance from "4" | 1.00 | 1.00 | 1.11 | Distance from "4" | 1.75 | 2.25 | 1.44 |
| Nixon | | | | Nixon | | | |
| Story treatment | 4.00 | 4.25 | 3.75 | Story treatment | 4.50 | 4.00 | 4.00 |
| Story favorability | 2.33 | 2.50 | 3.25 | Story favorability | 2.00 | 2.33 | 3.00 |
| Distance from "4" | 1.67 | 1.50 | .75 | Distance from "4" | 2.00 | 1.67 | 1.00 |

| McGovern | October | | | Total | | | |
|---|---|---|---|---|---|---|---|
| | ABC | CBS | NBC | McGovern | ABC | CBS | NBC |
| Story treatment | 4.46 | 4.12 | 4.18 | Story treatment | 4.54 | 4.41 | 4.11 |
| Story favorability | 5.23 | 5.18 | 4.88 | Story favorability | 5.18 | 5.38 | 5.09 |
| Distance from "4" | 1.23 | 1.18 | .88 | Distance from "4" | 1.18 | 1.38 | 1.09 |
| Nixon | | | | Nixon | | | |
| Story treatment | 4.08 | 4.00 | 3.88 | Story treatment | 4.12 | 4.06 | 3.87 |
| Story favorability | 2.97 | 3.10 | 2.50 | Story favorability | 2.71 | 2.82 | 2.80 |
| Distance from "4" | 1.09 | .90 | 1.50 | Distance from "4" | 1.29 | 1.18 | 1.20 |

[a]Represents mean score on a "1" to "7" scale where the value of the midpoint is "4.00" "1" equals most favorable to conservative, "7" equals most favorable to liberals.

the greater the distance from 4, the greater is the favorability to the candidate in question. ABC showed greater story favorability to Nixon than to McGovern except for the last sample-week cluster. CBS showed greater favorability to McGovern except for the first sample-week cluster. In the case of NBC, a change in story favorability from McGovern to Nixon in the October sample was great enough to make NBC's aggregate score show greater overall favorability to Nixon. On the story treatment dimension, NBC is also the only network to show conservative favorability at all.

Finally, we were able to generate an "embarrassment index" by working with the story favorability index. Stories coded as "6" or "7" (favorable to the liberals) with either the primary or secondary issue being the Republican party, and stories coded "1" or "2" (favorable to the conservatives) with either primary or secondary issue being the Democratic party were considered to be, by definition, "embarrassing" stories to the parties (and thus candidates) involved. This data is presented in Table 3-10.

Looking at the seven-week sample, ABC presented slightly more stories which embarrassed the Democrats than did NBC or CBS. This ABC figure becomes more important when we realize that ABC generally presents the fewest stories per broadcast of the three major networks. CBS presented approximately 50 percent more stories which were embarrassing to the Republicans than did ABC or NBC. In terms of semantic differential scoring, which attempts to tap substantive, narrated themes and consciously directed stories,[15] NBC generally had the most moderate, noncontroversial, and "nondirected" news coverage. The semantic differential technique as employed here is only one of a battery of possible techniques that could be employed to tap this dimension of television news coverage. While its application appears to have some merit, further refinements of this technique as well as the development of complementary measures does seem to be called for.

In terms of general coverage of major political and social issues, one important dimension that produced dissimilar results was our scoring for "hard" and for "soft" news. Given a limited amount of airtime, a general "philosophy" of news reporting is displayed by the proportions of airtime that a given network devotes to hard and to soft news. Hard news, the reporting of immediate and significant events, makes salient a different aspect of political reality than does soft news in which trends, background information, and so forth are reported. Table 3-11 presents hard news and soft news proportions for each network for each sample cluster and across all broadcasts.

We can see that across all sample weeks, while ABC and NBC utilized the same proportions of hard to soft news, CBS devoted more airtime to soft news than did its other two competitors. More interestingly, while across the sample weeks leading to the election the proportion of hard to soft news increased in the ABC and in the NBC formats, the amount of airtime in CBS broadcasts devoted to hard news *decreased*. Thus, in the closing days of the campaign, CBS

**Table 3-10**

**Embarrassment Index Scoring, Democratic and Republican Parties, Grouped and Aggregate Data**

| | July-August | | | September | | |
|---|---|---|---|---|---|---|
| | ABC | CBS | NBC | ABC | CBS | NBC |
| Democratic party | 9[a](4-5)[b] | 7 (5-2) | 4 (1-3) | 6 (2-4) | 3 (1-2) | 4 (1-3) |
| Republican party | 2 (2-0) | 11 (8-3) | 5 (4-1) | 5 (0-5) | 6 (4-2) | 3 (1-2) |

| | October | | | Totals | | |
|---|---|---|---|---|---|---|
| | ABC | CBS | NBC | ABC | CBS | NBC |
| Democratic party | 5 (2-3) | 7 (1-6) | 9 (5-4) | 20 (8-12) | 18 ( 7-11) | 19 (10-9) |
| Republican party | 13 (7-6) | 12 (6-6) | 9 (3-6) | 20 (9-11) | 29 (18-11) | 17 ( 8-9) |

[a]Number of stories defined as embarrassing.

[b]Numbers in parentheses represent contributions to the total from stories scored "1" and "7" on the story content-favorability scale followed by contributions to the total from stories scored "2" and "6."

Table 3-11

**Hard and Soft News Proportions of Airtime by Network for Sample Clusters and for Total Broadcasts**

| ABC | % Hard News | % Soft News |
|---|---|---|
| First sample-week cluster | 79 | 21 |
| Second sample-week cluster | 83 | 17 |
| Third sample-week cluster | 88 | 12 |
| Total broadcasts | 82 | 18 |
| **CBS** | | |
| First sample-week cluster | 80 | 20 |
| Second sample-week cluster | 80 | 20 |
| Third sample-week cluster | 74 | 26 |
| Total broadcasts | 77 | 23 |
| **NBC** | | |
| First sample-week cluster | 70 | 30 |
| Second sample-week cluster | 87 | 13 |
| Third sample-week cluster | 88 | 12 |
| Total broadcasts | 82 | 18 |

adopted a philosophy of "present the background, analyze the trends," which, given the limitations of total airtime, perforce restricted the amount of airtime that could be devoted to hard news stories.

### Summary Examples from Data: The Multidimensional Nature of News Broadcast Emphasis

The above data highlight the multifaceted nature of the broadcast messages transmitted via network evening news. Comparing message components for any given network shows wide ranges in programming style and emphases in format. We can present a thumbnail sketch of NBC to show this diversity, although such diversity is apparent in all network news presentations and NBC is chosen here simply as one illustration.

NBC gave the greatest amount of airtime coverage of all three networks to the Vietnam war, although within the Vietnam war categories ABC and CBS "out-reported" NBC on specific aspects of this conflict. NBC (as did ABC) presented more bloody "film themes" in its Vietnam war coverage, and NBC utilized the more powerful non-voice-over film more than did either ABC or CBS.

On the other hand, NBC's use of film coverage of domestic affairs, especially the coverage of Democratic and Republican party affairs, declined in proportion to CBS' use of non-voice-over film in covering these domestic issues. NBC gave McGovern the most "intimate" film coverage in terms of tightshot coding, but at the same time NBC of all three networks placed the greatest emphasis upon "Executive Agency Action." Furthermore, NBC, in terms of story treatment dealing with those "political" news stories, showed greater "semantic" and "thematic" balance than did CBS and ABC, and NBC's record in terms of "embarrassing stories" falls short of the number of such stories that CBS broadcast.

In short, the preceding discussion of findings should point out the lack of uniform "biasing" toward any particular political or personal statement on the part of any of the networks. On the other hand, within specific dimensions of the news messages we do find some interesting emphases and formatting decisions, even if these decisions are not clustered toward and/or uniformly favoring any political group of philosophy. It may well be the case, however, that different aspects of the broadcast message have different attitudinal effects upon different audience-types, and specific message dimensions in which cross-network and cross-issue variation were found should compel further political-communications research.

**Comparable New York Times Coverage**

Network news broadcasts are only one source of political information available to consumers of news. Daily newspapers, an alternative source of news, may provide substantially different coverage. We thus compared the news coverage of the television networks with that of a large metropolitan daily newspaper, the *New York Times.*

Direct comparison of print and electronic journalism is made difficult by the existence of a number of different constraints operating upon the networks and the *Times.* While both the networks and the *Times* are received by a national audience, the *Times* is much more subject to constraints imposed by local interest groups and the demands of its highly selective audience. We would expect, therefore, greater coverage in the *Times* of national and international events which are of particular importance to influential community members. As an example, we may see the *Times* devoting greater space to stories about the Middle East and other international items than any of the networks (in terms of percentage of total coverage).

All *New York Times* first-section news stories, except those dealing with issues local to the New York metropolitan area, were "forced choice" coded into the same forty-six possible "issue identification" categories that were used in coding television news stories. Local issues were defined as issues solely of relevance to residents of the New York metropolitan area such as corruption in the New York Police Department, City Council elections, local crime, and so forth. Issues of national importance such as school integration were included in our analysis. Issues of the *Times* were coded for the same Monday to Friday seven-week sample period as the TV news broadcasts in three clusters. No "secondary issue identification" was allowed, all coding decisions were based on headline and lead paragraphs. The number of column inches devoted to each story were measured to obtain a percentage of total coverage for each issue. No other dimensions, such as favorability, graphics, photographs, and so on, were coded. Thus comparison with TV news broadcasting is possible only on the basis of the proportional coverage of given issues within total coverage.

Over the seven-week sample, certain general tendencies are discernible. The *Times* devotes a higher percentage of its total national and international coverage to foreign news than even NBC which, of all the networks, tends to emphasize foreign news the most. This is a tendency which holds true for each of the sample-week clusters as well as for the total sample. Results are presented in Table 3-12 below. Note especially the striking difference between coverage on the domestic-foreign dimension by ABC and CBS and coverage by the *Times*. The large difference between these two networks and the *Times* in proportional presentation of domestic and foreign news also held true for each sample week.

Although the *Times* consistently devotes a higher percentage of its coverage to foreign news than any of the network evening news broadcasts, it consistently falls behind them in coverage of the Vietnam war as shown by Table 3-13.

While all the networks increased their Vietnam coverage over the three sample-week clusters, the *Times* showed a sharp drop in presentation of this issue from the first sample-week cluster (11.3 percent) to the second sample-week cluster (7.3 percent). The *Times* Vietnam coverage, however, almost tripled (18 percent) in the final sample-week cluster largely due to the announcement of and ensuring developments at the end of October concerning the Vietnam peace plan. In this respect, *Times* coverage most closely resembles that of ABC, which also nearly tripled its Vietnam coverage during this final preelection period.

**Table 3-12**
**Domestic and Foreign Affairs Coverage: ABC, CBS, NBC, and *New York Times***

|  | % Domestic | % Foreign |
| --- | --- | --- |
| ABC | 69.1 | 30.9 |
| CBS | 70.4 | 29.6 |
| NBC | 64.4 | 35.6 |
| *New York Times* | 56.2 | 43.8 |

Table 3-13

Vietnam War News Coverage by ABC, CBS, NBC, and the *New York Times* for a Seven-Week Sample Period

|  | % of Total News Coverage |
| --- | --- |
| ABC | 17.6 |
| CBS | 18.3 |
| NBC | 22.3 |
| *New York Times* | 13.2 |

A further comparison of the way in which the three networks and the *New York Times* covered the Vietnam war during our sample period is in terms of the three Vietnam issue categories which received the greatest coverage by each of these news sources. Table 3-14 shows the three most important Vietnam issues covered by each network and the *Times.*

It can be seen that the *Times'* top three Vietnam categories parallel somewhat those of the networks though at lower proportions of total news reporting. In percentage of total the *Times* most closely resembles CBS in its presentation of Vietnam stories. In both sources the same three categories receive the greatest coverage, in the same general order.

Further comparisons between the networks and the *Times* can be made in terms of percentage of coverage of non-Vietnam foreign news. Excluding the residual "Foreign Other" category, we found the top three stories for each news source on this dimension. The results are presented in Table 3-15.

While the top three categories closely parallel each other for the networks as well as the *Times* (this is also true within each sample-week cluster), it can be seen that the *Times* gives relatively greater space to each of these non-Vietnam foreign issues than any of the networks. In part, this can be accounted for by the *Times'* greater depth of foreign news in general.

In the presentation of domestic news issues by the networks and the *Times,* we compared the top five issues which received the greatest emphasis by each news source. The residual "Domestic Other" cateogry is excluded as well as "Democratic party" and "Republican party." (The latter two categories are covered later in Appendix A.) Table 3-16 presents the results of this comparison. Significantly, "Crime, Law and Order" and "Ecology" are the top two domestic issues covered by the *Times,* presumably issues of great concern to New Yorkers. While crime, and law and order also enter into the top five issues for all the networks, only NBC includes ecology as one of its most important domestic categories. Moreover, the *Times* is the only news source in our sample to give aggregated seven-week top-five coverage to issues concerning health, education and welfare, perhaps reflecting an urban bias in *Times'* reportage of news events.

Importantly, "Government Ethics" does not enter into the top five *Times'* domestic issues for the entire seven-week sample, while it assumes first place for

Table 3-14

Top Three Vietnam Issues and Percentage of Total Coverage for ABC, CBS, NBC, and the *New York Times* for a Seven-Week Sample Period

| ABC | | CBS | |
|---|---|---|---|
| Vietnam politics | (7.5%) | Vietnam politics | (6.3%) |
| Vietnam military | (5.2%) | Vietnam military | (4.4%) |
| Air war | (1.8%) | Vietnam other | (3.1%) |
| NBC | | *New York Times* | |
| Vietnam politics | (9.4%) | Vietnam politics | (6.2%) |
| Vietnam military | (4.9%) | Vietnam military | (3.4%) |
| Air war | (3.9%) | Vietnam other | (1.5%) |

Table 3-15

Top Three Non-Vietnam Foreign Issues for ABC, CBS, NBC, and the *New York Times* for a Seven-Week Sample Period

| ABC | | CBS | |
|---|---|---|---|
| Mideast | (3.4%) | Mideast | (2.8%) |
| Europe, N-NATO | (1.8%) | Europe, N-NATO | (1.8%) |
| Asia, NVM* | (1.7%) | Soviet-West relations | (1.0%) |
| NBC | | *New York Times* | |
| Mideast | (2.8%) | Mideast | (5.3%) |
| Asia, NVM | (1.9%) | Europe, N-NATO | (4.9%) |
| Europe, N-NATO | (1.7%) | Asia, NVM | (3.4%) |

*Asia, non-Vietnam related.

Table 3-16

Top Five Domestic Issues Covered by ABC, CBS, NBC, and the *New York Times* for a Seven-Week Sample Period

| ABC | | CBS | |
|---|---|---|---|
| Finance-economy | (4.9%) | Govt. ethics | (5.5%) |
| Govt. ethics | (3.6%) | Crime, law & order | (3.9%) |
| Crime, law & order | (2.8%) | Finance-economy | (3.6%) |
| Labor | (2.1%) | Civil rights | (2.0%) |
| Civil rights | (1.5%) | Military affairs | (1.9%) |
| NBC | | *New York Times* | |
| Govt. ethics | (3.3%) | Crime, law & order | (5.7%) |
| Finance-economy | (3.2%) | Ecology | (2.4%) |
| Crime, law & order | (3.2%) | Civil rights | (2.3%) |
| Labor | (2.6%) | HEW | (2.2%) |
| Ecology | (1.7%) | Finance-economy | (2.2%) |

CBS and NBC and second place for ABC in this sample. In the sample-week cluster of October-November, all three networks placed government ethics as their top domestic story; the *Times* during this period placed government ethics as its third most important story (though its proportional coverage of this issue [3.1 percent] is not significantly different from that of NBC [3.3 percent]). During the second sample-week cluster, all networks rated government ethics as the second most important issue while the *Times* rated it fifth. The Watergate incident and the Russian wheat deal account for most of the stories subsumed under this issue during these two sample-week clusters.

Finally, comparisons were drawn between campaign coverage of the Democratic and Republican parties. Seven-week percentages are presented in Table 3-17.

Unlike the measures applied to television news broadcasting in the making of political images, the measures of *Times* coverage of the presidential campaign do not indicate favorability to either candidate or to either party. Nonetheless, the significant fact to be drawn from the above table is the relatively smaller presentation given to the campaign by the *Times* as compared to the television networks. Moreover, the *Times* gave greater proportional reporting over the seven-week sample period to news about the Democratic party. This holds true for all the sample-week clusters except that of October-November just prior to the election when the *Times* gave greater column space to the Republican party (as did the TV networks).

From the first to the second sample-week clusters, the *Times* increased its coverage of the Republican party, but that of the Democratic party did not change significantly. Interestingly enough, its coverage of the Democrats dropped, though not significantly, during the third sample-week cluster. This trend is also true for the television networks, except for NBC which increased its Democratic as well as its Republican stories just prior to the election. We hesitate, however, to draw any final conclusions from these data concerning campaign presentation as the differences may not be statistically significant.

In summary, we reiterate the difficulty of direct comparison of the *Times* with the television networks because of the *Times'* greater general coverage of news events and the fact that in some cases, the networks differ as much among themselves as from the *Times*. Nevertheless, despite the different constraints operating on these two types of news sources, they are both subject to the ebb and flow of events, to somewhat equivalent limitations, that is, of space for the *Times* and of broadcast minutes for the television networks, and to the constraints of deadline reportage of the news. Given these similarities in the sources, we may note some consistent differences which remain between the *Times'* presentation of news and that of the television networks: (1) the *Times'* greater and more-in-depth coverage of foreign news, (2) the networks' relatively greater emphasis on Vietnam issues, and (3) the *Times'* greater coverage of certain domestic issues which, while of national importance, have reached a critical stage in the cities.

Table 3-17

Percentage of Coverage of Republican and Democratic Parties by ABC, CBS, NBC, and the *New York Times* for a Seven-Week Sample Period

|                  | ABC  | CBS  | NBC  | *Times* |
|------------------|------|------|------|---------|
| Democratic party | 17.9 | 16.9 | 15.5 | 9.8     |
| Republican party | 18.7 | 20.0 | 15.1 | 8.0     |

Of course, these differences in reporting between the networks and the *Times* reflect only differences in the manifest news content rather than differences in the perceptions of the audiences for each medium. Additional research will be required to assess the relative impact of the two media. As yet we have not compared the rapidly moving, transient visual story with the leisurely perusal or the same story in a newspaper which can be read or reread several times, or which can even be ignored if the headline is unappealing. Furthermore, we must develop techniques for measuring how members of the audience compare the credibility of words uttered by opinion leaders such as Walter Cronkite, John Chancellor, Harry Reasoner, and Howard K. Smith with words read in an anonymous press service report. Does the tone of voice of the newscaster, or his facial expression have an impact on the viewer which alters his perception of the "facts" in a news report? These and other aspects of the impact on the audience will have to be investigated if we are to compare not only the content but the impact of a given message on television with the same message presented in a newspaper.

## Comparison of News Reporting and Public Opinion Trends

Fortuitously for our research purposes, on four occasions during the summer and early fall of 1972, the Gallup Public Opinion organization polled its standard sample of American citizens and asked the question: "What do you think is the most important problem facing this country today?" It is possible to look at the results of these surveys and draw some very rough comparisons with the results of the first half of our television news content analysis.

In order to compare these data with our television sample, we have arranged the data into two groups, one prior to the period during which our television sample was taken and a second which parallels the first four weeks of our sample. At the time of this writing, comparable data are not available from the Gallup organization to compare the October and early November sample of television news.

Clearly, in order to demonstrate fully the effects of television news upon various audiences, a number of research controls and much more raw data would have to be available. Moreover, a longer time frame (to collect survey data and conduct further content analysis of news broadcasts) would be necessary to justify or validate fully any conclusions. As we do not have these additional data, our remarks will be kept to a minimum and all conclusions should be regarded as tentative.

The first issue we can concern ourselves with is the extent to which television news reports the general concerns of significant proportions of the news-watching audience. We can ask the consequent question as to whether or not television news *should* mirror the concerns of the news-watching audience.

The data are presented in Tables 3-18 and 3-19. Table 3-18 presents the proportions of people who mentioned the enumerated issues as the most important problems facing America today and the total proportion of airtime that the three networks devoted to these issues during the same time period. All data refer to the time period from "late July" to "late September," the time frames specified by the Gallup data.[16] Four of the sample weeks of television news that we analyzed are included in this time period.

While a number of concerns are reflected in relatively similar proportions of airtime news, there are some striking differences. Public concerns with crime and inflation far outdistance the amount of television news devoted to these subjects. Coverage of the war in Vietnam is of even greater concern to the American people than the relatively large amount of airtime devoted to this subject. However, it seems that the news audience could care less about international problems in general, and these types of stories are by far the most overrepresented in network news reporting.

For the most part, the data in Table 3-18 are only of heuristic value. The types of response categories used by the Gallup organization are different from the coding categories used in the television-news content analysis. Furthermore, respondents to the Gallup question were allowed to make multiple choices, thus somewhat obfuscating the resultant data. Nevertheless, the magnitude of the differences between the articulated concerns of the American people and the amount of airtime given to these same issues by network news cannot help but suggest that indeed there is a difference between what concerns the American people and what is reported as "important" (by virtue of inclusion) in nightly network news.

Of course, the data presented here are "static" in their design. It may well be the case that *eventually* concerns get translated into broadcast proportions. Time-series or time-lag data would be necessary to prove or disprove this point.[17] Such time-series data would have to be collected over a period of months, perhaps years, before the null hypothesis could be accepted. It is not inconceivable, for example, that the general emphasis on foreign affairs reflects long-standing interests and concerns of news editors which were fostered during

Table 3-18

**Proportion of Respondents Naming Given Issues as the Most Important Problem Facing America and Proportion of Television News Airtime Devoted to These Issues, by Network**

| Gallup Respondents | | ABC | CBS | NBC |
|---|---|---|---|---|
| Vietnam | 26.0% | 10.8% | 15.0% | 18.8% |
| Inflation | 25.0% | 3.8% | 3.9% | 4.1% |
| Crime | 9.0% | 3.4% | 5.5% | 3.7% |
| IR problems | 7.5% | 28.9%[a] | 30.3% | 33.9% |
| Ecology | 4.5% | 2.4% | 2.1% | 2.4% |
| Government ethics | 2.5% | 2.3% | 4.0% | 3.4% |

[a]Coded as all references to non-Vietnam foreign news stories from the television data.

the earlier "formative" years of these editors and which remained central to their scheme of things throughout the career-advancement process leading to their becoming news gatekeepers.

While we do not have such extensive data, it is possible to break the four-week parallel samples of Gallup respondents and television news coding into two separate sets. The Gallup surveys were conducted in late July and in late September. These time periods somewhat approximate our first two sample-week clusters so that we have near-simultaneous coding of the network news broadcasts during these periods.

As in Table 3-18, Table 3-19 presents parallel proportions of respondents who identified specific issues as the most important problems facing this country today and the proportions of total airtime devoted to these issues during roughly the same time periods. Sample-week cluster periods are identified with roman numerals "I" and "II," which correspond to the July-August sample and to the September sample, respectively.

Table 3-19 shows some preliminary trends across the two time periods under investigation. Due to the inherent weakness of the data, only the weakest of statistical techniques can be used to examine the results. We chose to use a variation of the binomial expansion which is appropriate for this type of analysis in place of the binomial formula when $N < 30$ (which is the case with the data in Table 3-19).

We observe that a rough directionality of change occurs in both the enumeration of the most important problem and in the proportions of airtime devoted to these general issues. Data are cited in Table 3-19 which exclude a collapsed HEW category from the Gallup data. There is some serious doubt as to the equivalence of this category across the survey research and the content analytic dimensions. Respondents' answers of "drug use," "poverty, and welfare" would have had to collapse into a survey-research HEW category, while in our coding dictionaries the HEW category included a number of other possible

**Table 3-19**

**Proportion of Respondents Naming Given Issues as the Most Important Problem Facing this Country Today, and the Proportion of Television News Airtime Devoted to These Issues, by Network (Results Cited for First and for Second Sample-Week Periods)**

| | Gallup data | | ABC | | CBS | | NBC | |
|---|---|---|---|---|---|---|---|---|
| | I | II | I | II | I | II | I | II |
| Vietnam | 25% | (↑)[a] 27% | 10.8% | (↓)[b] 10.8% | 12.1% | (↑) 17.8% | 17.2% | (↑) 20.4% |
| Inflation | 23% | (↑) 27% | 4.1% | (↑)[b] 4.1% | 4.4% | (↓) 3.3% | 3.8% | (↑) 4.5% |
| Crime | 10% | (↓) 8% | 5.0% | (↓) 1.8% | 5.5% | (↓)[b] 5.5% | 3.2% | (↑) 4.1% |
| IR problems | 5% | (↑) 10% | 31.2% | (↓) 26.6% | 23.7% | (↑) 36.8% | 30.8% | (↑) 37.0% |
| Ecology | 5% | (↓) 4% | 3.3% | (↓) 1.4% | 3.5% | (↓) .6% | 2.2% | (↑) 2.7% |
| Government Ethics | 2% | (↑) 3% | .1% | (↑) 4.4% | 2.6% | (↑) 5.4% | 4.0% | (↓) 2.7% |

[a] All arrows in parentheses signify direction of change between "I" and "II" measures.

[b] Direction of change ascertained by further carrying out of the decimal in order to eliminate "ties" in the data.

issues such as education, surgeon general reports on dangers of smoking, social security legislation and medicare, and so forth.

Working with directional changes in survey-research responses and in the results of our content analysis, we can generate relationships between the directions of change (an increased or a decreased interest) for given major issues and directions of change (increased or decreased coverage) for network airtime allocation. From the first to the second time periods, four issues increased in salience for the survey research respondents (hereafter referred to simply as "respondents") and two issues declined.

Across all networks, we "matched" increases or decreases in airtime allocation to increases or decreases in respondents' concerns. If both concern and airtime coverage increased, this was a "match." If concern and airtime coverage declined, we also considered this a "match." With an $N$ of 18 (18 possible matches), we found twelve matches across networks and across issues. Using a one-tailed test of significance, we ascertained that the probability of such a number of matches under the null hypothesis to be less than 0.10.[18] In other words, although causality cannot be attributed using such weak and incomplete data, interesting covariations do occur in terms of available data.

There are a number of competing explanations for even this level of parallel change. In the short run, the media may have shaped people's perception of what the salient issues were. This does not mean, however, that the media necessarily affected or changed people's attitudes or values concerning these issues. At the very least (if this explanation is correct), the network news *reinforced* perceptions of "what is important."

At the gross level described in Table 3-19, we argued that there are significant differences in the volume of what gets reported and in the relative concerns of the respondents with those issues. While it may be the case that in the long run the media do indeed mirror changes in public opinion, given the fact that these two time frames are only a few weeks apart, it is unlikely that the networks are aware of changes in public opinion as manifested in survey data and through interest articulation. If a causal arrow is someday to be assigned, our hypothesis would be that, at least over the short run, it will go from "media" to "public."

There may be another explanation which accounts for some of the variance. Any number of environmental and/or political-economic-social systemic variables may have direct impact upon people and their attitudes and values, that is, issues that they don't have to be "told about." Certain issues may become salient as a function of widespread economic changes, seasonal fluctuations, patterns of work and leisure, increased draft calls, or seasonal associations with past experience and with patterns of news reporting (such as the notion of "the long hot summers" and the urban riots that these summers produce). As an example, common street crime may have great personal importance to victims. Such events in themselves are not newsworthy; only policies directed toward the elimination of such crime are worthy of national attention.

Given these competing explanations, however, the argument that network news broadcasting has some impact upon public opinion seems at least plausible. Directional changes do co-occur in news reporting and in perceived salient news issues.

If we look at specific networks, several interesting observations can be made. For the respondents, concern with international problems (non-Vietnam) showed the greatest absolute percentage increase from the first to the second time periods. Likewise, for the two most widely-viewed networks, in this category we also encounter the greatest percentage increase of all categories between the two time periods. CBS had the fewest cases ($N = 1$) of deviance from public opinion trends (although again no causality is imputed here) and the networks with greater trend deviance, NBC and ABC, generally exhibited this trend deviance in specific general areas of news coverage. ABC "bucked" the trend in its international news coverage (Vietnam and international problems in general). NBC showed trend deviance in its domestic news coverage (crime, ecology, and government ethics). Across this time period, NBC increased its coverage of ecology and crime news, which the respondents did not consider as salient as they did in the first survey situation, and NBC decreased its coverage of government ethics although public interest in this issue continued to rise.

In four of the six cases, across all networks, where there was trend deviance between airtime allocation and degree of respondents' issue salience identification, we found that the *direction of change in the relative placement of stories in the deviating categories was the same as the direction of change in the issue salience.* Although such a level of analysis is precluded by the nature of the present data, these findings further suggest the probable impact of network news on attitude change or at least upon identification of issues as salient, and call for future application of multiple regression techniques to verify these tentative findings. The multiplicity of content categories used in this study, as well as the interesting variations in the use of these categories by the network news staffs, allow further explorations using regression techniques which should prove to be more powerful than working simply with limited descriptions of, and incomplete data from, television news messages.

# 4 Conclusion

This monograph has shown the many ways in which television news broadcasting transmits political messages to great numbers of citizen-audiences. A multidimensional coding scheme was generated and applied to the analysis of a sample of network news broadcasted during crucial stages of the 1972 presidential election campaign. We find some striking differences as well as some similarities in the news formats presented by ABC, CBS, and NBC during this seven-week sample period. Some of these general trends are as follows:

1. NBC consistently devoted more of its airtime to stories dealing with Vietnam and placed these stories earlier in the newscast than did CBS and ABC. Across the three sample-week clusters, all networks increased their coverage of the Vietnam war as the campaign progressed. ABC's increase in Vietnam war coverage was the most pronounced, with over 2-1/2 times as much coverage during the final sample-week cluster as during the first sample-week cluster.

2. CBS consistently devoted more airtime to the coverage of "domestic" stories than did either NBC or ABC, but all three networks concentrated upon roughly the same stories or story types. Government ethics was the big news issue during the campaign period, at least as presented by network television. CBS devoted approximately 50 percent more airtime to this issue across all seven sample-weeks than did ABC or NBC. Civil rights figured prominently in the domestic coverage of CBS and ABC. Surprisingly, among the "Top Five" domestic categories for NBC we do not find the topic of civil rights. However, unlike ABC and CBS, NBC did devote a relatively considerable proportion of its news to a current "peoples" cause, that is, ecology.

3. In terms of coverage of the two major political parties, CBS gave more airtime to the Republican party than to the Democratic party, while NBC and ABC gave slightly more coverage to the Democrats than to the Republicans. In all cases, however, the differences were not statistically significant. As a result of our sampling strategy, we were able to compare network news after both the Democratic and the Republican National Conventions. While the Democrats made more news after their convention, surprisingly, on ABC and NBC, they also made more news after the Republican Convention! This was the period of the Eagleton affair and its repercussions.

4. NBC consistently took the lead in reporting the "Air War" aspects of the Vietnam war, with over two times as much coverage than any other network. As the election came to a close, however, the third sample-week cluster shows

how effectively the Peace Talks developments and their political implications greatly cut the airtime devoted to the air war. Given a set airtime duration of between twenty and twenty-four minutes per broadcast, the additional news concerning the Peace Talks simply did not allow the airtime to cover other aspects of the Indochina war.

5. Concerning "non-Vietnam" foreign stories, the Mideast received by far the most attention. Surprisingly, the problems in Northern Ireland, while making the "Top Three" news categories during the first sample-week cluster, did not receive as much attention in the subsequent sample clusters. Of all three networks, CBS gave the most time to Soviet-American relations, but this coverage was for the most part the result of the Wheat Deal stories, a government ethics emphasis by CBS that has been discussed above. Comparing reporting of stories dealing with the Mideast, one can observe a central thesis of this monograph. While, for example, CBS and NBC devoted the same amount of airtime to this issue (as measured across the entire seven-week sample), the story placement for NBC was consistently "lower" (i.e., the stories appeared earlier in the broadcast). Looking at the October sample and comparing ABC and NBC, while ABC gave more airtime to the Mideast, the story placement score for Mideast stories on NBC was almost 33 percent lower.

Given the known importance of serial order of presentation as a determining factor of attributed significance and the persuasive power of earlier-presented arguments in attitude change, it must be argued that simple allocation of airtime alone to various story-types is a less-than-satisfactory estimate of the content (and importance) of network news.

There are subtle messages in network news broadcasting that can be tapped only through the use of sophisticated, multidimensional coding techniques and content categories. We find, for example, that during the 1972 presidential election in which an incumbent president (an executive) is running against a senator (a legislator), network news broadcasts devoted between two and three times as many stories to executive activities as it did to legislative activities. Although the legislature was not in session during much of our sample period, future research can focus on the relative coverage of the executive and legislative branches of government when they are in session, and its potential impact on public conceptions of the distribution of power in government.

There are also subtle messages concerning the candidates themselves. Camera angles and degree of tightshot coverage in film of candidate activities also show marked differences across time and, to some extent, across the networks. CBS generally portrayed Nixon as more intimate, approachable, warm, and "big" than did ABC and NBC, although all three networks generally gave McGovern the "tighter" coverage. Looking at the NBC tightshots after the September sample in which both Nixon and McGovern were given identical tightshot coverage, we see a major change in the October sample, with Nixon losing the intimacy and warmth of tightshot coverage.

We also find differences in candidate time with voters on film and candidate speaking time on film. It is very difficult to compare Nixon and McGovern scores given the fact that Nixon used a series of "proxies" during the campaign period.[1] However, comparing vice-presidential candidates, we find some interesting differences. Across the seven-week sample, Agnew is given far more film time in which he is speaking on issues than is Shriver, but with the exception of CBS, Shriver is shown with the voters three to four times as long on broadcast newsfilm than is Agnew. Part of this difference may be attributed to campaign style, but we may also speculate that the networks, chastised by Agnew in 1969 for, among other things, paraphrasing remarks made by administration officials, were careful to avoid misquoting Agnew.

We see similar differences in types of film used in Vietnam war coverage, in "bloodiness" of film themes from the war zone, and across a host of different dimensions of television news coverage. In short, the presentation of political reality by network news broadcasts is a complex and subtle affair. This monograph has simply shown the extent of the network differences (and, in some cases, similarities), and has presented some highly interesting data along key dimensions.

At this point, two major questions remain: (1) Given the type of analysis conducted here, can one then argue that the networks are "biased" in their coverage of political reality? (2) What is the *impact* of news broadcasting and of its various dimensions upon specific types of audiences or upon the American populace in general?

The answer to the first question is relatively simple: Due to the necessary encoding of all possible "news" into a 20+ minute nightly format, some sort of selection process is inevitable. This should not be perjoratively labeled bias, however, because "bias" implies that the possibility to be "unbiased" actually exists (which in the case of putting together an evening news program is simply not the case).[2]

Even in terms of the patterns of and motivations behind selective encoding, this study cannot be used to draw inferences about the encoding process, itself. As Klein and Maccoby[3] and more recently, Meadow[4] have argued, levels of campaign aggressiveness as well as role incumbency (or lack thereof) do generate different amounts of "raw news" and without a complete understanding of the news-generating process (which is discussed earlier in this monograph) as well as a handle upon the "candidate news output," the social scientist cannot possibly ascertain the objective level and direction of differential encoding.[5]

If one wanted to get to the real question of selective encoding, one would have to return to the model of Figure 1-1 and expand the analysis of "news-generating sources" as well as the analysis of available news-input channels to the working news headquarters in New York City. Such a tentative model is presented in Figure 4-1, although the problems of access to data and of operationalizing the necessary indicators are of course immense, perhaps insurmountable.

The second question, that of the impact of television news upon specific audiences or upon the population in general, is a much more difficult question to answer. The initial portions of this monograph have attempted, through a theoretical overview of communications in politics and through a critical review of research to date on the effects of mass media, to show in a nonquantitative manner the effects of mass media not only upon individual attitudes and values but also the actual distribution of political power within a political system.

It is argued that the ability to control the channels of communication within a political system, the ability to limit the types and numbers of individuals and groups who have access to the communication process, potentially constitutes a major resource of political power.[6] Television news, even in a "nonswitched" format, at least allows access to coverage to groups whose political notoriety would otherwise be minimal. With the advent of cable television and highly specialized "news" programs of a switched variety,[7] the impact upon political power distribution promises to be significant.

It is further argued that, even controlling for the impact upon the distribution of political power within a given political system, television news takes on additional political significance as a function of the additional speed of encoding and transmission, the greatly increased size of audience and the vividness of messages afforded by television broadcasting. Television as a tool of communication is significantly more powerful than earlier nonelectronic tools and consequently will grow in political power and importance.

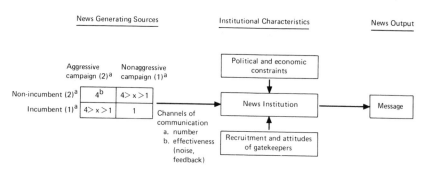

[a]Ordinal difference in news generating potential controlling for other variable.

[b]Ordinal amount of newsworthy statements necessary to wage an aggressive or non-aggressive campaign.

**Figure 4-1.** Model of News Flow from Event to News Available to Viewer.

At the theoretical levels of systems analysis and communication flow, television news appears to maximize the impact of political communications within a given polity. Actual quasi-experimental and experimental attempts to quantify this impact have been hindered in the past by a number of methodological and theoretical problems. The "two-step flow" arguments, which suggest a minimal role for mass-communications effects and which posit primarily peer-group and community-opinion leader influence were found to be unconvincing and/or inappropriately applied.

It is argued in this monograph that opinion leaders who constitute the intervening step in the two-step flow may indeed be the news commentators themselves. We must therefore reformulate our conception of the two-step flow and reconsider just who the opinion leaders are. The networks themselves recognize this opinion leadership position of their commentators, advertising for example, that "Walter Cronkite is the most trusted man in America."

Truly valid research of this sort would necessarily entail a much more rigidly controlled research design which would take into account audience characteristics, differential "use" of television news by different audiences and social-psychological types, long-term media effects, the input from other information sources, and a distinction between television news as possibly *changing* attitudes and values or simply reinforcing already held attitudes and values (the latter case leading not to different attitudes and values but rather to a higher "activation" in terms of political action). We are now in the process of generating data which should complement the findings and the message-analysis protocol reported here.

We do have some preliminary data that suggest a possible importance of the effects of television news broadcasting. A comparison of changing trends in Gallup survey-research responses to the question of "The most important problem facing America today," with changing trends in network news topic-coverage shows parallel movements in these two trends. However, no exogenous variables are controlled in the present study, "within-society differences" are not investigated, and the data analyzed are treated as relatively weak "ordinal" data.

In summary, we do find wide variance both within network programming across news-message dimensions and across network formatting itself. Many of our results, however, especially in light of new evidence as to the importance of mass-media effects, do show striking news coverage emphases. Again, these emphases are not all in the same "political direction" nor are all dimensions of any given network "oriented" in exactly the same way.

Further research must be conducted using this multisensory, multichannel message-analysis protocol. Moreover, the whole question of differential audience effects caused by different message components must be further studied. Especially in terms of the "grammar of film," a hitherto unexplored news-message dimension, we find major examples of vividly portrayed news emphasis which must be taken into account in any future research design.

A few final words should be addressed to the continuing controversy of liberal bias in the network evening news. As stated above, subjective political philosophies and associated orientations interact with the imperatives of the news-reporting situation which force the collapsing of the evening national news-reporting into a twenty-odd minute newscast. The "gatekeepers" who must make story selections and choose presentation angles under intense time pressure cannot be faulted for selecting those political stories and interpretations they deem as most newsworthy in terms of their personal and philosophical orientation. Moreover, the professional ethics of news reporting act as an objectifying "check" on the newsman's personal opinions.

During the 1972 presidential campaign, the Republican and Democratic parties were given roughly the same amount of airtime coverage by all the networks but the placement of stories dealing with the Democratic party usually appeared earlier in the newscast. This, of course, says nothing about the content of the various news stories. Stories of government ethics (the Watergate affair) continually were given a predominant place in domestic coverage although it is an untested empirical question as to whether such coverage would have been as extensive had the problems of government ethics been linked to Democratic party activities. The agency-action data that show a preponderant emphasis on "executive activity" can be considered a network bias in favor of the incumbent president who in this case happened to be a Republican. It is an untested empirical question as to whether this emphasis would have been greater or perhaps less had the incumbent been a Democrat. A comparable study of an election period in which the incumbent is a liberal Democrat would be necessary to draw sound inferences relating to bias from the data of this study.

As regards the coverage of the presidential and vice-presidential candidates, McGovern and Shriver were given in certain news-dimension aspects more favorable treatment than were Nixon and Agnew. McGovern was shown more on film both with voters and making political statements than was Nixon, and McGovern was presented in more intimate and "warm" tightshot coverage light than was the president. Again, however, we see the interaction of a number of possible encoding variables including political preference of the newsmen and editors, the type of campaign that President Nixon conducted, the necessary aggressiveness of a challenger campaigning against an incumbent, and so forth. Agnew was definitely presented as a talker while Shriver was presented as a crowd-pleaser. If any bias occurs here it could be the function of two prior political conditions: (1) the types of images that both men wished to portray (for example, with Agnew perhaps consciously making more "newsworthy" statements than Shriver), and (2) the predispositions of the newsmen involved in candidate coverage when and if these predispositions were at variance with the objective behavior of the candidates. Democratic party film coverage was somewhat more extensive than Republican party coverage, although the difference in means is not statistically significant.

Story treatment and story favorability scores, as established through the use of our semantic differential scales, show a very slight liberal bias, although the difference is not statistically significant. In story treatment and story favorability scores for McGovern and Nixon stories alone, ABC and NBC actually presented Nixon in a better light than they do McGovern, although the difference is slight. CBS, which across our different semantic differential techniques did present McGovern in a more favorable light than Nixon, also was the one network broadcasting a preponderant number of stories which could be considered "embarrassing" to Nixon and/or the Republican party. However, this emphasis did not hold across all three networks.

Comparison of *New York Times* news coverage on those message dimensions it shared with network news electronic journalism showed a high level of convergent validity between print and electronic news coverage, with the *Times* coverage (on these similar dimensions) being most similar to CBS news coverage. This compatibility generally corresponds with the "liberal" position the *New York Times* favors on a wide variety, but not all, of salient domestic and foreign political issues.

Many scholars have found what seems to be a certain liberal bias in network news coverage. *Our limited data, reflecting the unique characteristics of the 1972 election campaign period, does not demonstrate bias existing uniformly across all message dimensions.* Measurable bias appears to be a function of a series of antecedent factors ranging from personal political preferences to newsman accessibility to a news story and the actual political realities that are there to be reported. Our sample is too small to come to any precise conclusion other than that some message emphases probably do exist. A parallel study to the present effort conducted during the incumbency of a political liberal could be matched with our findings from 1972 and the resultant conclusions could be much different or much more pronounced. Such a parallel study, of course, awaits the unfolding of future history and the development of electoral realities which would make such a comparable study possible.

The present study has shed some light on the message characteristics and variations in these characteristics which occurred during the unique 1972 campaign period. We also believe the present study has advanced the general methodology of TV-newscast content analysis. The substantive results are interesting in themselves, but of equal importance is the notion that multiple streams of evidence, multiple coding, and variations in the recruitment and training techniques of coders can and have been explored during the continuous methodological developing of this research project.

The problems of formulating precise coding criteria that can be consistently and uniformly applied by human coders may perhaps never be completely solved. With low levels of precoding training, the chances for coder error or at least different coding patterns will increase. On the other hand, with extensive coder training the possibility exists that the coders will adhere faithfully to the coding preferences, orientations, and perceptions of the research design. Nevertheless, techniques have been suggested in this study and have been utilized in our research that minimize as far as has been done to date the possible effects of coder bias in the analysis of the television news.

These same techniques should be applied to a wider range of television news data, both longitudinally across time and laterally to include news specials, television magazines, and so forth. At the same time, campaign and noncampaign periods should be compared and contrasted in terms of news coverage of events and issues. We hope the research reported here can eventually be compared with a noncampaign analysis. Different findings might very well have emerged if the news sample had been noncampaign, or if the campaign had been conducted under different political circumstances (e.g., an incumbent liberal Democrat). Finally, we would suggest that such techniques and such comparisons be extended to include not only the national news broadcasting in one nation's TV net but instead be expanded into a series of cross-national, comparative media and political projects.

It is our hope that we have advanced the state of understanding of the characteristics of the TV broadcast message. Nevertheless, it is obvious that much more research is needed in these and other closely related intellectual concerns in the general field of politics and communications.

# Appendixes

# Appendix A: Television
## News-Coding Protocol

A brief listing of some of the quality control we have used should be informative to the reader. Coders were selected after careful screening, which included the answering of a twenty-page questionnaire that tapped media use, prior evaluations of media credibility, educational background, political attitudes and values, political and social awareness (through identification of important historical and political figures and through the measurement of familiarity with current sociopolitical issues), a history of childhood and subject's family media use, and so forth. Four coders were eventually selected so that the coding staff has a balance on certain key variables. (One person never watched television news, one person always did. One person felt that television news was a credible source, another did not. One person characterized himself as politically liberal, another characterized himself as politically conservative, and so on.) Two males and two females were chosen. All were white, one was foreign-born although thoroughly acculturated. Three of the four coders are presently pursuing graduate degrees in communications, history, and education-linguistics.

Although we attempted to achieve a balanced coding staff, further "randomizing" procedures were employed. Coders worked and made decisions in two-person teams. The team dyads were changed and mixed frequently. No individual or team coded primarily any one network's news broadcasts.

Prior to the actual coding, extensive training was conducted in which the coders were familiarized with the coding instrument. "Reliability levels" were established and scores taken which assured us of the coding proficiency of the selected coders. Coding was done continuously throughout the project. Coding fatigue was eliminated by limiting the time of continuous coding.

Reliability levels generally ranged around 0.80 to 0.85 for intracoder reliability. Due to the complexity of the indices involved,[1] as well as the failure of previous studies to attain this high a level of quality control, we are satisfied with the obtained reliability levels.

1. *Date Identification*

2. *Network Identification:*  ABC = 1, CBS = 2, NBC = 3.

3. *Issue Identification, Secondary Issue Identification:* Each story and editorial is scored along an issue-type dimension: twenty-one foreign issues plus a "foreign other" and twenty-three domestic issues plus a "domestic other" category are coded. Each story is given a code according to the category which applies (see Table A-1). The central theme of the story or editorial is coded as the "issue identification." A second score may be coded *optionally* if there is a second theme or news issue explicitly involved in the story. Generally, a reporter's allusion to or the mention of such a secondary issue by an individual in the story is the criterion used to determine whether this dimension is

applicable. Secondary issues are aspects that are ancillary to the central news story, and the final distinguishing characteristic of secondary (as opposed to primary) issue identification is its airtime in relation to the primary issue. In other words, its airtime must be less than that given to the central theme.

If two issues are alluded to at the same time during the broadcast of a given story or editorial, the predicating issue is coded as the primary one. For example, a story in which women's liberation and abortion themes are *simultaneously* discussed and in which no thematic *airtime* distinctions are possible, would have as its issue identification "women's liberation" and "abortion" as its secondary issue identification.

4. *Story Placement, Story Place:* Position in the serial order of presentation of a given story in a total news broadcast. The first story in the broadcast is coded as 1, the second story in the broadcast is coded as 2, the third story as 3, and so on.

A broadcast with a greater number of stories will have more story placements thus overloading certain story means. Therefore, the number of stories in a broadcast is "controlled" by dividing every story placement score by the number of stories in that broadcast. For example, in a news broadcast of 14 stories, the *controlled story placement* score would be 3/14 for the third story of the broadcast, 8/14 for the eighth story in the broadcast, and so on.

5. *Airtime Allocation, Story Duration*: In seconds, the length of airtime given to a particular story.

6. *Story Graphic*: The visual display of a photograph, map, emblem, or caption behind the anchorman during a studio presentation or during the voice-over segment of a field reporter's coverage of an event. The duration of airtime showing a story graphic is coded in seconds as well as the number of story graphics presented.

During preelection coverage, each network often displayed a general graphic denoting campaign coverage, such as CBS's "CAMPAIGN '72." These were not coded as graphics. Campaign graphics were defined so as to include only those representing a specific event or candidate. ABC's striped button bearing the name of a candidate is an example.

Three other conditions were held to apply to the coding of graphics. Maps or partial maps of the United States were not coded as story graphics, for unlike maps of foreign countries or cities, they possess less information content for American viewers and, unlike logos or artistic representations, less symbolic content.

Artists' drawings of trials and participants in trials in which photographs were not permitted were coded as graphics, their being less than film but still an attempt by the network to present something more than verbal reportage of an event.

Finally, caption format was taken into consideration in coding the number of graphics presented. If a number of graphics and/or captions following the same

**Table A-1**
**Coding Manual 1**

| *Foreign* | *Domestic* |
|---|---|
| 1. POW'S | 22. Labor news |
| 2. Air war | 23. Finance, economy (other) |
| 3. Domestic response, anti-war activity | 24. Inflation |
| 4. Vietnam politics, war diplomacy | 25. Unemployment |
| 5. Vietnam military | 26. Wage and price controls |
| 6. Congress response, democratic | 27. Ecology |
| 7. Congress response, Republican | 28. Consumer affairs |
| 8. Congress response, general | 29. Welfare rights |
| 9. Vietnam, other | 30. Abortion |
| 10. NATO, Western Europe | 31. Health, Education, Welfare (other) |
| 11. Western Europe, non-NATO | 32. School busing |
| 12. Ireland | 33. Government ethics |
| 13. Soviet Blod (intra) | 34. Critique of Gov't secrecy and/or military secrecy |
| 14. Soviet Bloc, Western Bloc (inter) | 35. Defense overruns |
| 15. Soviet Bloc, Third World (inter) | 36. Republican party |
| 16. China | 37. Democratic party |
| 17. Mideast | 38. Third parties' activities |
| 18. Other Asia, Vietnam related | 39. Farms |
| 19. Other Asia, non-Vietnam related | 40. Civil rights |
| 20. Africa (non-Mideast) | 41. Women's liberation |
| 21. Latin America | 42. Urban problems (transit and housing) |
| | 43. Military affairs |
| | 44. Crime, law and order |
| | 45. Other |
| | 46. Other, foreign |

format were displayed in a given story, these were counted as one graphic. In the coverage of McGovern's speech to the Wall Street stock broker's organization, for instance, the CBS reporter presented a field report in which the major points of McGovern's address were displayed consecutively as captions on the screen. While the informational content of each caption (graphic) was different, the *graphic format* itself and the inferred intent of that format did not change. Therefore, all these captions were coded together as one graphic along with their total summed time of presentation.

7. *Voice-over Film*: Film shot at the scene of the news and broadcast during the news program in which a narrator who is not seen on the film reports on the action shown in the film. The number and duration of voice-over film clips are coded. Voice-over film mitigates against letting the film "speak for itself," and the narrator tells the audience what is being seen on, or implied by, the film. Thus film is considered "voice over" only if the narrator is a reporter, and narration by a participant in an event, for example, a passenger on a train that has been in a wreck, is coded as "non-voice-over" *and* "non-candidate statement." Short reference: *VO film*.

8. *Non-Voice-over Film*: Similar to voice-over film with the important difference that no reporter narration accompanies the film. The film and the events

portrayed "speak for themselves," and news commentary during the film is absent. This category is similar to the *cinema verité* technique and assumes similar viewer impact.

Film segments in which candidates and/or non-candidates (story relevant individuals) make a statement or are interviewed are also coded as non-voice-over film in that the film clip here also speaks for itself, that is, no network or reporter explanation, analysis or comment is given. Short reference: *NVO film*.

9. *Field Report*: Film in which the reporter on the scene is shown on camera making a statement about the news story. Situations in which the reporter appears as an interviewer, however, are not so coded, the interviewee's statement being the focus of the coverage in this case rather than the reporter's questions, explanation, comment, or analysis. Like VO and NVO film clips, number and airtime duration of field reports are coded.

10. *Commercial Proximity*: Stories are coded along the dimension of (1) being broadcast immediately before a commercial, (2) being broadcast between commercials, (3) being broadcast immediately following a commercial, and (4) being broadcast in a format in which none of the first three conditions holds. The assumption here is that commercial proximity and/or type of commercial with which a story is sequentially associated may be the result of specific intent on the part of a network. To date, however, no analysis of this dimension has been conducted.

11. *Noncandidate Interview or Statement Film Segment*: Type of noncandidate and duration of film are coded. Types of noncandidates are identified and, in sequential order, first noncandidate, second noncandidate, and mixes of first and second types of noncandidates are scored. There are two types of possible mixes: mixes of first type of noncandidate, and mixes of first and second types of noncandidates. For example, (1) in a news story in which a Democratic senator, a consumer advocate, and another Democratic senator are interviewed in sequential order, the first senator would be the first noncandidate, the consumer advocate would be the second, and the other senator a mix of the first noncandidate. (2) If a senator, a consumer advocate, and a labor leader were interviewed in sequential order, the labor leader would be coded as a mix of the first and second noncandidates.

In reality, the great majority of stories broadcast include no more than two or three noncandidate interviewees, and these generally fall into two of the given coding categories for noncandidates (see Table A-2) so that the three slots provided for statements by such individuals are, for the most part, sufficient. Obviously, more than two types of noncandidate interviewees in any given story are not coded. This situation was very rarely encountered. In such cases, the third type of interviewee was perforce coded as a mix of the first two. While there may be some loss of specificity, this second mix category does tap the degree and sequential placement of network presentation of a variety of viewpoints and public figures.

**Table A-2**
**Coding Manual 2**

1. Bystander
2. Nonfamous story-relevant individual
3. Spokesman for local organization (Floridians for Nixon, etc.)
4. Spokesman for national political organization, nongovernmental
5. Spokesman for labor union
6. Spokesman for big-business community
7. Spokesman for ecology, consumer groups
8. Spokesman for antiwar movement
9. Spokesman for Pentagon
10. Spokesman for civil rights group
11. Senator, Republican
12. Senator, Democrat
13. Congressman, Republican
14. Congressman, Democrat
15. Spokesman for administration, cabinet officer, present or past administration
16. Spokesman for governmental agency, including state agency
17. Local political unit spokesman (nonfederal)
18. Family member in family role
19. Campaign Staff (takes priority over #15)
20. Other

(Second Spokesman)
21. Bystander
22. Nonfamous story-relevant individual
. . .
. . .
. . .
40. Other spokesman

(Mixes)
77. Mixes of first spokesman
88. Mixes of first and second spokesman

12. *Candidate Coverage*: This category is coded whenever a presidential or vice-presidential candidate appears on film, even if only in a tangential way, for example, in stories concerning state and local political races, a network might show a few seconds of a presidential candidate endorsing a local official (see Table A-3).

13. *Crowd Coverage*: Size and reaction of "crowd" viewing or mixing with a candidate. Crowd is here defined as a group of potential voters whose support (votes) the candidate is attempting to win. This excludes reporters as at a press conference, but includes, for example, the Wall Street stockbrokers' organization. In the case of a press conference, a cabinet meeting, or a campaign staff meeting, crowd coverage is not coded at all.

In some cases, estimates of crowd size and reaction were based upon a reporter's explicit statement. Where the size and/or emotional reaction of a crowd was indiscernible, a neutral classification was scored. If a crowd was

**Table A-3**
**Coding Manual 3**

1. At home, with family
2. On vacation
3. Mixing with blacks
4. Mixing with other ethnic groups
5. Visiting shops
6. With children
7. At airport
8. In urban setting, campaigning (when other categories do not apply)
9. In rural setting, campaigning (when other categories do not apply)
10. Contemplating, or surmising with friends
11. Contemplating, or surmising with reporter
12. Speaking at formal meeting
13. Speaking at informal meeting, candidate elevated
14. Speaking at informal meeting, candidate at audience level
15. Candidate private meeting with running mate
16. Candidate speaking in presence of running mate
17. Candidate speaking with running mate on film at least one-third of time
18. Candidate endorsing local officials (formal)
19. Candidate being endorsed by local officials (formal)
20. Candidate being endorsed by nongovernmental individual or group (formal)
21. Candidate endorsing local officials (formal)
22. Candidate being endorsed by local officials (informal)
23. Candidate being endorsed by nongovernmental individual or group (informal)
24. Candidate being endorsed, not present
25. In office or headquarters
26. Other
27. Formal press conference

known to be present, but was not shown on film, this dimension was not coded.

The emotional reaction of the crowd was measured in terms of applause, vocal expression and facial expressions shown on camera. Hostility, while seldom shown on camera, tended to consist of heckling by members of a audience listening to a candidate. In cases where a few hecklers were heard among a large group of people, the crowd was coded as having a mixed reaction to the candidate. The nonemotional category was reserved for crowds in which no specific reaction was discernible.

14. *General Candidate Activity*: A "yes-no" dimension which records whether the candidate is engaging in general activity ("campaigning in Oshkosh") or is shown in activities specifically related to a political issue.

The criterion here is the delineation by the candidate or the network of a specific issue to which the candidate speaks or a specific audience, such as members of the AFL-CIO, with whom the candidate is engaging in some activity. This dimension is always coded when a candidate appears on film. Where his activity is indeterminate, it is coded as nonspecific.

15. *Film Time, Candidate Statement*: In seconds, broadcast airtime is coded in which the candidate appears on film and makes a statement or is interviewed.

16. *Film Time, Candidate with Voters*: In seconds, broadcast airtime is coded in which the candidate is shown on film mixing with voters, that is, shaking hands, conversing with people in a crowd, and so forth. This does not include film in which the candidate is speaking to an audience of voters from a podium, nor does it include shaking hands with local officials on the way to the podium. Voters are here defined as unidentified people in unofficial roles with whom the candidate mixes.

17. *Tightshot Coverage*: Tightshot coding identifies the distance of the camera shot from the presidential and vice-presidential candidates who appear on film. Tightshot coding is scored along a seven-point scale, ranging from camera shots which show only the candidate's head to film in which the candidate is shown not in a crowd and at a distance. Positive weighting is given to close-up film of only a candidate's hands or if the camera angle is shooting upward. Negative weighting is given to film in which the camera angle is shooting down on the candidate. With the exception of the "lowest" category (coded 1), which represents the least tightshot (candidate at a distance, not in a crowd), the highest tightshot category that applies is coded for the film sequence. All film clips of candidate activity are coded as a unit. Tightshot scoring is *not* conducted on every piece of candidate film footage in a sequence. The limiting unit is the story. With two *different* stories in which a candidate is shown on film, two tightshot scores are established, one for each story. (See Table A-5).

18. *Candidate Association*: This category is used when film is broadcast showing a candidate in close association or contact with identifiable others.

The candidate may be presented to an audience by a local official, may be shown on a platform with a senator, or may be presented as talking with staff or cabinet members. In these cases, candidate association is coded. For this dimension to be coded, it must be shown by the film that the candidate is engaged in some activity with this other individual(s). Senator Kennedy presenting candidate McGovern to a New York City rally would be so coded, but a group of local officials on the side lines of an airport meeting would not.

19. *Hard News and Soft News*: Each story is scored along a hard news/soft news dichotomy. Hard news is defined as news which would be dated or inappropriate if broadcast the following day. Soft news, therefore, is news which

**Table A-4**
**Coding Manual 4**

90. Large crowd, friendly
91. Large crowd, mixed
92. Large crowd, hostile
93. Large crowd, apathetic
94. Medium-sized crowd, friendly
95. Medium-sized crowd, mixed
96. Medium-sized crowd, hostile
97. Medium-sized crowd, apathetic
98. Under-attended crowd, friendly
99. Under-attended crowd, mixed, hostile, or apathetic

**Table A-5**
**Coding Rules for the TV News Category of Tightshots**

7 = Shows *only the candidate's head* more than in just passing (e.g., for four or five seconds duration)

6 = Shows the candidate's head and only the top of his shoulders for at least four or five seconds. Can include filming him in a crowd where *momentarily* the cameraman is jostled further away from the candidate making for a slighly less tight film shot.

> Note: Categories 6 and 7 may be distinguished by the further criterion of being consciously planned and filmed shots vs. haphazard glimpses of the candidate. Indeed, what we are trying to determine is the extent and nature of consciously different candidate coverage.

5 = Shows the candidate from the middle of the chest at least 75% of the time.

4 = Shows the candidate from the waist up at least 75% of the time.

3 = Shows the candidate from the waist up less than 75% of the time, but does not show any distant shots of the candidate (distant shots here defined as film in which the candidate's image, his body, is less than half the size of the television screen. If this type of shot is used and category 1 does not apply, code 2.)

2 = Shows relatively distant shots where candidate's image, his body is partially blocked by crowds (e.g., walking among the voters) at least 50% of the time.

1 = Shows distant shots where entire candidate's body is present (e.g., walking alone or with few individuals) and unblocked.

> Note: This category is the inverse of 6 and 7. If there are no tight-tight shots (6 or 7), and if category 1 occurs consciously at all, code the film clip as 1.

0 = No shots of candidate.

*Weighting Factor for Camera Angle:*
If the Film of the Category You Have Chosen to Code Has at Least 33% of the Following Camera Angles, Add or Subtract One Point in the Following Directions.

Add one point: camera is below candidate shooting upward
Subtract one point: camera is above candidate shooting down

For example, film shows candidate from the abdomen up at least 75% of the time (coded as "5") but cameraman is filming down on the candidate (camera shot from above the horizontal [cameraman standing, candidate sitting], change the code from a "5" to a "4". Maximum Value for Tightshots = Eight ("7" + "1" for weighting).

Hands: When there are shots of the candidate's hands only, also weight by a factor of 1. But do not weight doubly if there are both shots of candidate's hands alone and also of candidate from above. Maximum value is still 8.

Nota Bene: Code the Highest Category Which Applies for All the Candidate Film.

---

need not be broadcast on a given program in order to be interesting and/or topical. A story about a specific plane crash would be hard news, while a story about the problems of airport overcrowding (with no reference to a specific plane crash, FAA ruling, or other event from the news day) would be a soft news story.

20. *News Commentary*: For all stories with the exception of editorials or editorial comments, the amount and nature of commentary is scored as "extended," "present," or "absent." Extended commentary is defined as some prognostication about the implications of an event for the future. Present commentary is defined as an interpretation of the event or actions of individuals excluding future implications. Thus a reporter's remarks concerning the probability of McGovern's winning New York State are coded as extended commentary, while his comment that New York voters are, for instance, "apathetic" would be coded as present commentary. The use of value-laden objectives is often a clue for coders in this category. While a reporter's coverage of an event or state of affairs may be supported by percentage figures and references to sources of news, his interpretation of those figures or sources of news in terms of his own (i.e., not quoted from other sources) adjectival or other description is considered commentary. Moreover, in all cases commentary is considered to consist of "information" presented by the reporter which is not substantiated by reference to quoted sources or which is not obvious to or inferrable by the viewer from a filmed presentation.

Distinctions are also made between commentary from the field reporter and commentary from the in-studio anchorman. In filmed presentations, commentary is generally found in the concluding field report. In fact, it was found that field reports are often reserved for just this purpose.

21. *Secondary Commentary*: Identical to news commentary but coded separately and used in those cases in which there is a chronologically second commentary on the news. For example:

(1) In a given story, there may be extended field commentary from a reporter at some point in a story and additional extended or present commentary from the anchorman at the end of the story. The anchorman's commentary would be coded as secondary commentary.

(2) In a given story, there may be present commentary by the field reporter during a segment of voice-over film. The field report at the end of the same story may also include extended commentary by the reporter. His final remarks would thus be coded as extended secondary commentary.

The coding unit for commentary is generally the topic about which implications or interpretations are being presented. Thus an instance of commentary may consist of a few adjectives ("X abandoned his usual mild mannered stance") or of several sentences ("X will take New York if he can garner the votes of labor leaders and if . . . ") In the coding of commentary an attempt was made to describe both extended and present commentary if both were included in a story. Thus, if there were sequentially two instances of present commentary and one of extended commentary, one unit of present and one unit of extended commentary were coded.

22. *Editorial*: News editorials or comments are scored according to the individual who makes the editorial. Thus NBC generally presents editorials in the form of "David Brinkley's Journal;" on ABC Howard K. Smith or Harry

Reasoner presents an editorial at the end of each news broadcast; Eric Sevareid is the usual editorial commentator for CBS. Editorials are scored along all the same dimensions as regular news stories except the commentary categories since the editorial form presupposes some sort of comment. (See Table A-6.)

23. *Agency Action*: Those stories in which the issue in the news entails some agency action are coded accordingly. For example, if there is a story about Congress' passing a welfare rights bill, "welfare rights" would be the issue identification and Congress as an agency initiating the action would be coded along the agency-action dimension. Thus we have a measure not only of which issues are covered by the news but, moreover, which sectors of government are reported as "most active" by the news broadcasts. (See Table A-7.)

Executive action, including agencies and representatives of the executive branch, is perhaps the most difficult to define. In these cases, all reportage of executive agencies "doing something" which could conceivably have further consequences was coded as agency action. The formal or informal sphere of an agency's influence or legal responsibilities was the second factor taken into account for the coding of executive agency action. Thus President Nixon's engaging in trade talks with Japan was coded as agency action, but not his spending a weekend in Key Biscayne. The General Accounting Office's issuance

**Table A-6**
**Coding Manual 5**

|   |
|---|
| 1 = Howard K. Smith |
| 2 = Harry Reasoner |
| 3 = Other, ABC |
| 4 = David Brinkley |
| 5 = Other, NBC |
| 6 = Eric Sevareid |
| 7 = Other, CBS |

**Table A-7**
**Coding Manual 6**

1 = Supreme Court action
2 = Congress action, general
3 = Senate action
4 = House of Representative action
5 = Presidential action, includes executive branch operations (Justice Dept., Council of Economic Advisors, Kissinger and National Security Council, Wage and Price Control agencies, etc.)
6 = Lower court, either federal or state, action
7 = Governmental agency action (e.g., FCC, TVA, FDA, FTC, etc.)
8 = State executive action
9 = Local government action, all levels nonfederal except state executive and state courts
0 = No action agent

of a report is action by an agency since analysis rather than decision-making is GAO's only function. Henry Kissinger's meetings in Paris were coded as agency action even if no discernible result was reported since Kissinger's job is presumably to facilitate rather than to make decisions.

24. *Story Content Favorability*: A seven-point semantic differential scale is used to assess the favorability of each story's content to a conservative or liberal position. Each story is scored from a 1 for story content most favorable to the conservative position to a score of 7 for story content which is most favorable to a liberal position. The coding team can choose to code the story at any number within the 1 to 7 range. The midpoint is 4. If the story content is favorable to neither the conservatives or liberals, or equally favorable to both, a score of 4 is assigned. If the story is slightly more favorable to the liberals, a 5 is assigned, if slightly more favorable to conservatives, a 3 is assigned, and so on throughout the scale.

In most cases, *content* favorability is relatively clear cut, for example, an enthusiastic reception for McGovern in Massachusetts is, in content, favorable to liberals; Congress' upholding of a Nixon presidential veto is in general favorable to conservatives. There are some cases, however, in which a greater degree of coder judgment is called for. While we are not assessing viewer impact, but rather differential network presentation of news events, some implicit judgments about impact and intent must be made in coding this dimension. Such judgments whenever possible were avoided. Thus a story about Vice-President Agnew's being heckled could be construed (either as to impact or intent) as rude behavior on the part of liberals (favorable to conservatives) or as demeaning to Agnew's image and thus favorable to liberals. In such cases, a 4 was assigned to story content favorability since interpretation would have to be based on viewer's or presenter's political positions.

In cases which were not so ambiguous, other criteria were used to assess content favorability, such as general principles of morality. Thus initial reportage of the Watergate buggings was coded as unfavorable to conservatives (in that Republican personnel were allegedly engaged in these activities and Republicans are generally or popularly viewed as more conservative than liberal across a wide range of issues). Coverage of a story about alleged American firestorms in Vietnam was coded as favorable to liberals on the same basis.

In all cases, content favorability was coded on the basis of the "informational theme" of the story, for example, "Senator Eagleton formerly underwent psychiatric treatment," rather than reportorial commentary on the implications of this news. In this case, content would be coded as unfavorable to liberals based on the fact that mental illness is in general negatively valued rather than based on any implications a reporter may draw from this fact.

If, however, the *event* reported is one of McGovern's campaign staff *stating* that Eagleton's former illness will react badly on the McGovern campaign, content is coded as unfavorable to liberals on the basis of the explicit statement that it is unfavorable.

Finally, "unfavorable to conservatives" is considered to be equivalent to "favorable to liberals" and vice versa. Thus stories unfavorable to conservatives, but not necessarily favorable to liberals are coded as if favorable to liberals, that is, between 5 and 7. A case in point is pollution of waterways by large industries. This is favorable to liberals, but not necessarily unfavorable to conservatives except insofar as conservatism is associated with big business.

25. *Story Treatment Favorability*: A distinct coding dimension for network *treatment* of a story is coded. Each story, as with content favorability, is coded using a semantic differential scale with 1 as most favorable to conservatives and 7 as most favorable to liberals.

Treatment includes such aspects of presentation as the amount and kind of film shown, the time given to interviewee's statements or to the statements of a speaker, types of individuals given airtime, amount and kind of commentary, and portions of a story given emphasis. In part, this dimension is a function of many other characteristics of news presentation that are coded independently and formally on other dimensions of the protocol. However, treatment favorability, unlike these other dimensions, is an attempt to measure negative or positive affect transmitted and/or intended to be transmitted by a network. It is of particular importance given the possibility that favorable or unfavorable treatment may be independent of content favorability.

In order to minimize coders' own biases—a problem inherent in utilizing this kind of dimension—we adhered to "values" of the treatment aspects mentioned above. Thus the story of alleged American initiated fire storms in Vietnam was coded as neutral in treatment favorability because, other things being equal, interviews with individuals on both sides of the issue were shown. If only an interview with a Pentagon official had been shown, treatment would have been coded as favorable to conservatives since the issue (event) was clearly one of opposing viewpoints. However, even if two sides of an issue are presented, if substantially greater interview, statement, or reportage time is given to representatives of one position, treatment favorability will reflect this by a coding of something other than 4.

Differential emphasis on various aspects of a story are also included in treatment favorability. Thus, in the preelection revelation of a Vietnam peace plan, CBS gave greater emphasis (in time and verbiage) than ABC and NBC to the possible problems with President Thieu that might conceivably result in the execution of such a plan. Other things being equal, CBS's treatment of this story would be coded as somewhat favorable to liberals, that is, unfavorable to conservatives because the potential ensuing peace was made to appear less certain than would appear from the simple presentation of events and quoted sources.

Duration and kind of film were also taken into account in coding this dimension. Thus substantial footage of Agnew's enthusiastic reception by the voters of Los Angeles and of his speech to them would account for some degree of favorability to conservatives. While comparison of stories was avoided in the coding process, it did enter into the coding of treatment favorability when obvious differences appeared in sequential stories. If, for instance, the above Agnew-favorable story were immediately followed by a short, and on other dimensions, less favorable McGovern story, treatment of the McGovern story would be coded as unfavorable to liberals on the basis of duration and juxtaposition.

Finally, soft news, because it is "unnecessary," was assumed to have, by definition, a liberal or conservative bias on treatment dimension if its content favorability was biased. For example, a soft news story concerning the polluting of the Great Lakes by large industries would be coded as unfavorable to conservatives (big business) in content and also in treatment as the network presenting the story made the decision to devote time to the issue.

It should be noted, however, that in cases of hard news, content and treatment favorability may go in opposite directions on the semantic differential scale. If a story concerning the Watergate incident is treated dispassionately and matter-of-factly, its treatment score will be neutral (4), while its content score will probably favor the liberals.

26. *Vietnam Action Visuals, Secondary Vietnam Action Visuals*: Film themes are coded when film from Indochina and/or the Vietnam war are broadcast on the news. Using a supplementary coding manual, scoring is accomplished using the same strategy described above in the issue identification, secondary issue identification scoring. Film themes and not film narration are scored. Scoring ranges from 1 for Vietnamese population in daily routine, no violence or results of violence show, through progressively more violent and/or bloody and/or destructive film themes. The upper limit in this protocol is film showing maimed, napalmed, diseased, and/or dead civilians.

A few of the above categories merit further explanation. For category 4, "Soldiers in operation, no enemy contact," soldiers must be shown engaging in military activities or on a military base rather than, for instance, sightseeing in Saigon. They may be on maneuvers, marching in formation, repairing equipment, and so forth. In category 6, "Results of air war," the film shown must be known (from reporter's commentary) to be immediately or clearly related to, and a result of, bombing rather than other types of battle or military action. The same holds true for category 8, "Results of North Vietnamese terror;" it must be somewhere stated or otherwise demonstrated that the footage shown is the result of North Vietnamese terrorism. Such results would include homeless people, fatherless children as well as the destruction of, or damage done to, crops, fields, homes, and other buildings.

Assignment of a portion of Vietnam film presented to primary or secondary Vietnam action visuals was generally based on duration of the theme. If, for instance, thirty seconds of air-war footage is followed by ten seconds of wounded soldiers, air war would be coded as first action visual and wounded soldiers as secondary action visual. In some cases only first action visual is coded, for example, coverage of a Vietnamese holiday in Saigon might present film of

**Table A-8**
**Coding Manual 7**

---

0 = No Vietnam visuals
1 = People living, no violence
2 = Battle scene, desolate or near desolate, shows destruction
3 = Soldiers in operation, no enemy contact
4 = Soldiers in operation, enemy contact
5 = Wounded soldiers
6 = Results of air war (e.g., smoke from napalm, planes in action); must be temporarily immediate or clearly air-war related
7 = Dead bodies or "lifeless" wounded or gory wounded
8 = Results of North Vietnam terror (includes damage to civilian areas as a result of mortars)
9 = Wounded or napalmed civilians, maimed children

---

category 1 only. In some stories, however, emphasis may replace duration as the criterion for first or second coding. This usually occurs where film shows wounded and/or dead bodies. For example, ten seconds of film of a screaming, wounded child would be coded as first action visual even if the same piece of film contained thirty seconds depicting soldiers in operation with enemy contact.

27. *Time Attended Dead or Wounded; Time Covered Dead; Time Unattended Dead*: Used in conjunction with the Vietnam action visuals, these interrelated categories are scored when film from Indochina is broadcast on the evening news. Where the Vietnam action visuals identify film themes, time attended dead or wounded, time covered dead, and time unattended dead measures, in seconds, the airtime duration of the news broadcast in which film is shown portraying individuals or bodies in the appropriate conditions which qualify for these three categories.

28. *Political Embarrassment Measure*: While not a distinct coding dimension, the political embarrassment measure is an operationalization of the concept of the embarrassing news story, using the story-content favorability measure described above. If a story is coded as having a *content* favorability highly favorable to the liberals, but either the primary or secondary issue identification of the story is coded as "Republican Party," the story is considered as "embarrassing" to the Republicans. Likewise, if the story is coded as highly favorable to the Republicans but the story is coded as primary or secondary issue identification dealing with the Democrats, then the story is considered as "embarrassing" to the Democrats. Computerized sorting and cross-tabulation procedures are used to retrieve and correlate this aspect of our data.

# Appendix B: Initial Coding Staff Evaluations of News Coverage of Specific Issues

Please answer all questions by circling or writing in the appropriate number.

NAME    TOTALS; N=4

Please Answer the First Set of Questions with Respect to Your Situation Since Coming to College.

1. From which source do you usually obtain most of your national news?
   1.** Television    2. Radio    3.** Newspapers    4. Magazines
   5. Other:

2. Do you currently own or have regular access to a television?
   1.*** Yes   2.* No

3. If you watch one of the network dinner-hour news programs, which network do you usually watch?
   1.* ABC    2.* CBS    3.* NBC    4.* Don't Watch

4. During the past week, did you watch the same network news show three or more times?
   1.** Yes    2. ** No   3. Don't Watch

5. If you regularly watch a second network dinner-hour news program, which network do you usually watch?
   1. ABC    2. CBS    3.** NBC    4.* Don't Watch

6. Which newspaper(s) are you most likely to read on an average day?
   **Inquirer;    *Bulletin;    *New York Times;    *None

7. Would you classify yourself as a regular viewer (typically watching the same network news show three or more times per week)?
   1.** Yes    1.* No    3.* Didn't Watch

8. As you were a youngster, say between 4 and 12 years old, on the average how prominent was television viewing in general (not just news) in your family setting?
   1. *TV was but even present
   2. *Present but not at all prominent
   3. **Somewhat prominent

4. Quite prominent
5. Fundamental to family setting

Please Use the Following List for Answers to the Next Set of Questions. Write In the Number of Your Answer on the Line to the Left of the Question. List First and Second Choice.

1. Underground newspaper
2. Weekly news magazine (e.g. Time, Life, Newsweek)
3. Monthly news magazine (e.g. New Republic, Harper's National Review
4. Local radio news broadcast
5. Local radio talk show
6. Network television news broadcast
7. Local television news broadcast
8. Network news specials, documentaries, etc. (e.g., *Sixty Minutes*, *First Tuesday* )

9. Which would you say is, in general, the best source of national news?  2\*; 3\*\*; 6\*\*; 8\*\*
10. Which would you say is, in general, the best source of local news? 4\*\*\*; 7\*\*\*
11. Which would you say is the most reliable and accurate source of news about the war in Southeast Asia?  3\*\*; 6\*; 7\*; 8\*\*
12. Which would you say is the most reliable and accurate source of news about the 1972 election campaign?  2\*\*; 6\*\*; 7\*; 8\*
13. Which is your own most important source of political news;  2\*; 4\*; 6\*; 7\*
14. Which is your own second most important source of political news? 2\*; 3\*; 4\*; 8\*
15. Which is your own third most important source of political news? 1\*; 6\*; 7\*; Other\*
16. "Network television news has been basically fair in its reporting of political events."
    1. Strongly Agree
    2. \*\*\*Agree
    3. \*Disagree
    4. Strongly Disagree

17. "The network television news programs have presented a fair picture of the domestic debate over the war in Southeast Asia." 2\*; 3\*\*\*
18. War protestors should try to capitalize on television coverage of protest activities to propagandize for their own positions." 2\*\*\*; 3\*
19. "Network television newscasters should be _____ editorial interpretations of the news."

1. Banned from making
2. **** Allowed to make
3. Encouraged to make
4. Required to make

20. On the average, how many days of the week do you usually watch at least one regularly scheduled news program?

    1   2**   3   4   5*   6   7*

Please Use the Following Answer Categories to Indicate the Level of Your Interest In the Issues and Concerns Listed Below. Write the Number of Your Answer on the Line Provided to the Left of the Item:

1. Very Interested.
2. Mildly Interested.
3. Distantly Interested.
4. Not interested in this topic.

21. 1.75* Paris Peace Talks
22. 1.75 Racial Conflicts
23. 1.50 The Draft
24. 2.00 Middle East Conflict
25. 1.00 American Election Campaign
26. 2.00 People's Republic of China
27. 2.00 Ecology and Pollution
28. 1.75 Phase II Economic Policy

29. 2.00 Conflict in Northern Ireland
30. 1.00 War in Southeast Asia
31. 1.00 Nixon Administration
32. 2.50 Philadelphia Politics
33. 1.75 Prisoners of War
34. 1.50 Students
35. 1.75 Mass Media
36. 2.00 Military Spending

*Mean scores are inserted.

## Indicate Your Personal Evaluation of the Following News Persons:
### *David Brinkley*

| | | | | | | | | | |
|-----|-------------|-----|-------|-------|-------|-------|------|-----|---------------|
| 37. | Impartial   | 1   | 2*    | 3     | 4     | 5**   | 6    | 7*  | Partial       |
| 38. | Unbiased    | 1   | 2*    | 3     | 4*    | 5*    | 6*   | 7   | Biased        |
| 39. | Accurate    | 1*  | 2**   | 3     | 4*    | 5     | 6    | 7   | Inaccurate    |
| 40. | Interesting | 1   | 2*    | 3     | 4*    | 5     | 6*   | 7*  | Uninteresting |
| 41. | Balanced    | 1   | 2*    | 3*    | 4*    | 5*    | 6    | 7   | Unbalanced    |
| 42. | Complex     | 1   | 2**   | 3**   | 4     | 5     | 6    | 7   | Simple        |
| 43. | Tough       | 1   | 2**   | 3     | 4**   | 5     | 6    | 7   | Soft          |
| 44. | Emotional   | 1   | 2     | 3     | 4*    | 5     | 6**  | 7*  | Logical       |
| 45. | Strong      | 1   | 2*    | 3*    | 4**   | 5     | 6    | 7   | Weak          |
| 46. | Active      | 1   | 2*    | 3***  | 4     | 5     | 6    | 7   | Passive       |
| 47. | Efficient   | 1*  | 2**   | 3*    | 4     | 5     | 6    | 7   | Bungling      |
| 48. | Popular     | 1*  | 2     | 3**   | 4     | 5*    | 6    | 7   | Unpopular     |
| 49. | Intelligent | 1*  | 2***  | 3     | 4     | 5     | 6    | 7   | Unintelligent |
| 50. | Liberal     | 1   | 2**   | 3     | 4**   | 5     | 6    | 7   | Conservative  |
| 51. | Sensitive   | 1   | 2**   | 3*    | 4*    | 5     | 6    | 7   | Insensitive   |

## Indicate Your Personal Evaluation of the Following News Persons:
### *Howard K. Smith*

| | | | | | | | | | |
|-----|-------------|-----|-------|-------|-------|-------|------|-----|---------------|
| 52. | Impartial   | 1   | 2     | 3*    | 4**   | 5     | 6    | 7*  | Partial       |
| 53. | Unbiased    | 1   | 2     | 3**   | 4*    | 5     | 6*   | 7   | Biased        |
| 54. | Accurate    | 1   | 2*    | 3*    | 4*    | 5*    | 6    | 7   | Inaccurate    |
| 55. | Interesting | 1   | 2     | 3     | 4**   | 5*    | 6*   | 7   | Uninteresting |
| 56. | Balanced    | 1   | 2*    | 3*    | 4*    | 5*    | 6    | 7   | Unbalanced    |
| 57. | Complex     | 1   | 2     | 3**   | 4*    | 5     | 6    | 7*  | Simple        |
| 58. | Tough       | 1   | 2**   | 3*    | 4*    | 5     | 6    | 7   | Soft          |
| 59. | Emotional   | 1   | 2     | 3*    | 4*    | 5     | 6**  | 7   | Logical       |
| 60. | Strong      | 1   | 2*    | 3**   | 4*    | 5     | 6    | 7   | Weak          |
| 61. | Active      | 1   | 2*    | 3**   | 4*    | 5     | 6    | 7   | Passive       |
| 62. | Efficient   | 1*  | 2     | 3**   | 4     | 5     | 6*   | 7   | Bungling      |
| 63. | Popular     | 1   | 2*    | 3*    | 4**   | 5     | 6    | 7   | Unpopular     |
| 64. | Intelligent | 1   | 2*    | 3**   | 4     | 5     | 6*   | 7   | Unintelligent |
| 65. | Liberal     | 1   | 2     | 3     | 4*    | 5*    | 6*   | 7*  | Conservative  |
| 66. | Sensitive   | 1   | 2*    | 3     | 4*    | 5*    | 6    | 7*  | Insensitive   |

**Indicate Your Personal Evaluation of the Following News Persons:**
*John Chancellor*

| | | | | | | | | |
|---|---|---|---|---|---|---|---|---|
| 67. | Impartial | 1 | 2 | 3* | 4* | 5** | 6 | 7 | Partial |
| 68. | Unbiased | 1 | 2 | 3* | 4** | 5* | 6 | 7 | Biased |
| 69. | Accurate | 1 | 2*** | 3* | 4 | 5 | 6 | 7 | Inaccurate |
| 70. | Interesting | 1 | 2*** | 3* | 4 | 5 | 6 | 7 | Uninteresting |
| 71. | Balanced | 1 | 2* | 3** | 4* | 5 | 6 | 7 | Unbalanced |
| 72. | Complex | 1 | 2** | 3** | 4 | 5 | 6 | 7 | Simple |
| 73. | Tough | 1 | 2* | 3* | 4** | 5 | 6 | 7 | Soft |
| 74. | Emotional | 1 | 2 | 3 | 4* | 5** | 6* | 7 | Logical |
| 75. | Strong | 1 | 2* | 3* | 4** | 5 | 6 | 7 | Weak |
| 76. | Active | 1 | 2*** | 3* | 4 | 5 | 6 | 7 | Passive |
| 77. | Efficient | 1 | 2*** | 3* | 4 | 5 | 6 | 7 | Bungling |
| 78. | Popular | 1 | 2** | 3* | 4* | 5 | 6 | 7 | Unpopular |
| 79. | Intelligent | 1 | 2**** | 3 | 4 | 5 | 6 | 7 | Unintelligent |
| 80. | Liberal | 1 | 2** | 3 | 4** | 5 | 6 | 7 | Conservative |
| 81. | Sensitive | 1 | 2** | 3 | 4** | 5 | 6 | 7 | Insensitive |

**Indicate Your Personal Evaluation of the Following News Persons:**
*Walter Cronkite*

| | | | | | | | | |
|---|---|---|---|---|---|---|---|---|
| 82. | Impartial | 1 | 2 | 3 | 4* | 5*** | 6 | 7 | Partial |
| 83. | Unbiased | 1 | 2 | 3 | 4** | 5** | 6 | 7 | Biased |
| 84. | Accurate | 1 | 2* | 3** | 4* | 5 | 6 | 7 | Inaccurate |
| 85. | Interesting | 1 | 2* | 3 | 4* | 5** | 6 | 7 | Uninteresting |
| 86. | Balanced | 1 | 2 | 3** | 4** | 5 | 6 | 7 | Unbalanced |
| 87. | Complex | 1 | 2* | 3* | 4* | 5* | 6 | 7 | Simple |
| 88. | Tough | 1 | 2* | 3 | 4** | 5* | 6 | 7 | Soft |
| 89. | Emotional | 1 | 2 | 3* | 4** | 5 | 6* | 7 | Logical |
| 90. | Strong | 1 | 2* | 3 | 4*** | 5 | 6 | 7 | Weak |
| 91. | Active | 1 | 2* | 3** | 4* | 5 | 6 | 7 | Passive |
| 92. | Efficient | 1 | 2* | 3** | 4* | 5 | 6 | 7 | Bungling |
| 93. | Popular | 1* | 2** | 3 | 4* | 5 | 6 | 7 | Unpopular |
| 94. | Intelligent | 1 | 2** | 3* | 4* | 5 | 6 | 7 | Unintelligent |
| 95. | Liberal | 1 | 2 | 3 | 4**** | 5 | 6 | 7 | Conservative |
| 96. | Sensitive | 1 | 2 | 3** | 4** | 5 | 6 | 7 | Insensitive |

## Indicate Your Personal Evaluation of the Following News Persons:
### Harry Reasoner

| | | | | | | | | | |
|---|---|---|---|---|---|---|---|---|---|
| 97. | Impartial | 1 | 2* | 3 | 4* | 5* | 6 | 7* | Partial |
| 98. | Unbiased | 1 | 2* | 3 | 4* | 5* | 6 | 7* | Biased |
| 99. | Accurate | 1 | 2* | 3* | 4* | 5* | 6 | 7 | Inaccurate |
| 100. | Interesting | 1* | 2 | 3* | 4* | 5* | 6 | 7 | Uninteresting |
| 101. | Balanced | 1 | 2 | 3* | 4*** | 5 | 6 | 7 | Unbalanced |
| 102. | Complex | 1 | 2* | 3** | 4* | 5 | 6 | 7 | Simple |
| 103. | Tough | 1 | 2** | 3 | 4** | 5 | 6 | 7 | Soft |
| 104. | Emotional | 1 | 2 | 3* | 4* | 5* | 6* | 7 | Logical |
| 105. | Strong | 1 | 2** | 3 | 4** | 5 | 6 | 7 | Weak |
| 106. | Active | 1 | 2** | 3** | 4 | 5 | 6 | 7 | Passive |
| 107. | Efficient | 1 | 2* | 3** | 4* | 5 | 6 | 7 | Bungling |
| 108. | Popular | 1 | 2* | 3* | 4** | 5 | 6 | 7 | Unpopular |
| 109. | Intelligent | 1 | 2** | 3* | 4* | 5 | 6 | 7 | Unintelligent |
| 110. | Liberal | 1 | 2* | 3 | 4** | 5 | 6* | 7 | Conservative |
| 111. | Sensitive | 1 | 2* | 3 | 4*** | 5 | 6 | 7 | Insensitive |

## On the Scales Below Please Indicate Your Personal Opinion of How Network Television News, in General, Treats the Following Issues and Topics:

### People's Republic of China

| | | | | | | | | | |
|---|---|---|---|---|---|---|---|---|---|
| 127. | Complete | 1 | 2 | 3* | 4 | 5 | 6*** | 7 | Incomplete |
| 128. | Unbiased | 1 | 2 | 3* | 4** | 5 | 6* | 7 | Biased | 4.5 |
| 129. | Accurate | 1 | 2 | 3* | 4** | 5* | 6 | 7 | Inaccurate |

### Middle East Conflict

| | | | | | | | | | |
|---|---|---|---|---|---|---|---|---|---|
| 130. | Complete | 1 | 2* | 3** | 4 | 5* | 6 | 7 | Incomplete |
| 131. | Unbiased | 1 | 2 | 3 | 4* | 5** | 6* | 7 | Biased | 4.167 |
| 132. | Accurate | 1 | 2 | 3 | 4 | 5** | 6** | 7 | Inaccurate |

### Nixon Administration

| | | | | | | | | | |
|---|---|---|---|---|---|---|---|---|---|
| 133. | Complete | 1* | 2** | 3 | 4 | 5 | 6* | 7 | Incomplete |
| 134. | Unbiased | 1 | 2* | 3* | 4** | 5 | 6 | 7 | Biased | 2.92 |
| 135. | Accurate | 1 | 2** | 3* | 4* | 5 | 6 | 7 | Inaccurate |

### Military Spending

| | | | | | | | | | |
|---|---|---|---|---|---|---|---|---|---|
| 136. | Complete | 1 | 2 | 3 | 4* | 5** | 6* | 7 | Incomplete |
| 137. | Unbiased | 1 | 2 | 3* | 4* | 5** | 6 | 7 | Biased | 4.58 |
| 138. | Accurate | 1 | 2 | 3 | 4** | 5** | 6 | 7 | Inaccurate |

### Students

| | | | | | | | | | |
|---|---|---|---|---|---|---|---|---|---|
| 139. | Complete | 1 | 2 | 3 | 4 | 5* | 6*** | 7 | Incomplete |
| 140. | Unbiased | 1 | 2 | 3* | 4 | 5** | 6* | 7 | Biased | 4.92 |
| 141. | Accurate | 1 | 2 | 3* | 4** | 5 | 6* | 7 | Inaccurate |

### War in Southeast Asia

| 142. | Complete | 1 | 2** | 3 | 4* | 5* | 6 | 7 | Incomplete | |
| 143. | Unbiased | 1 | 2* | 3 | 4 | 5*** | 6 | 7 | Biased | 3.58 |
| 144. | Accurate | 1 | 2** | 3 | 4* | 5* | 6 | 7 | Inaccurate | |

### Ecology and Pollution

| 145. | Complete | 1 | 2 | 3 | 4 | 5*** | 6* | 7 | Incomplete | |
| 146. | Unbiased | 1 | 2 | 3* | 4** | 5* | 6 | 7 | Biased | 4.00 |
| 147. | Accurate | 1 | 2* | 3*** | 4 | 5 | 6 | 7 | Inaccurate | |

### Paris Peace Talks

| 148. | Complete | 1 | 2** | 3 | 4 | 5* | 6* | 7 | Incomplete | |
| 149. | Unbiased | 1 | 2** | 3 | 4** | 5 | 6 | 7 | Biased | 3.25 |
| 150. | Accurate | 1 | 2* | 3** | 4* | 5 | 6 | 7 | Inaccurate | |

### Mass Media

| 151. | Complete | 1 | 2 | 3* | 4 | 5** | 6* | 7 | Incomplete | |
| 152. | Unbiased | 1 | 2 | 3* | 4 | 5* | 6** | 7 | Biased | 4.67 |
| 153. | Accurate | 1 | 2 | 3* | 4* | 5** | 6 | 7 | Inaccurate | |

### Prisoners of War

| 154. | Complete | 1 | 2* | 3 | 4 | 5** | 6 | 7* | Incomplete | |
| 155. | Unbiased | 1 | 2 | 3** | 4** | 5 | 6 | 7 | Biased | 4.00 |
| 156. | Accurate | 1 | 2 | 3* | 4*** | 5 | 6 | 7 | Inaccurate | |

### Racial Conflicts

| 157. | Complete | 1 | 2 | 3* | 4 | 5* | 6** | 7 | Incomplete | |
| 158. | Unbiased | 1 | 2 | 3* | 4*** | 5 | 6 | 7 | Biased | 4.167 |
| 159. | Accurate | 1 | 2 | 3** | 4* | 5* | 6 | 7 | Inaccurate | |

### Phase II Economic Policy

| 160. | Complete | 1 | 2** | 3 | 4 | 5* | 6* | 7 | Incomplete | |
| 161. | Unbiased | 1· | 2* | 3* | 4* | 5* | 6 | 7 | Biased | 3.5 |
| 162. | Accurate | 1 | 2 | 3*** | 4* | 5 | 6 | 7 | Inaccurate | |

### The Draft

| 163. | Complete | 1* | 2* | 3* | 4 | 5* | 6 | 7 | Incomplete | |
| 164. | Unbiased | 1* | 2** | 3 | 4 | 5* | 6 | 7 | Biased | 2.75 |
| 165. | Accurate | 1 | 2** | 3* | 4 | 5* | 6 | 7 | Inaccurate | |

### Conflict in Northern Ireland

| 166. | Complete | 1 | 2 | 3** | 4 | 5** | 6 | 7 | Incomplete | |
| 167. | Unbiased | 1 | 2** | 3 | 4* | 5 | 6* | 7 | Biased | 3.67 |
| 168. | Accurate | 1 | 2* | 3* | 4* | 5* | 6 | 7 | Inaccurate | |

### The Viet Cong

| 169. | Complete | 1 | 2* | 3 | 4 | 5* | 6* | 7* | Incomplete | |
| 170. | Unbiased | 1 | 2 | 3 | 4 | 5*** | 6 | 7* | Biased | 5.167 |
| 171. | Accurate | 1 | 2 | 3* | 4 | 5** | 6 | 7* | Inaccurate | |

*American Election Campaigns*

| 172. | Complete | 1* | 2* | 3* | 4 | 5 | 6* | 7 | Incomplete | |
|------|----------|-----|-----|-----|------|------|-----|---|------------|------|
| 173. | Unbiased | 1 | 2 | 3* | 4** | 5* | 6 | 7 | Biased | 3.58 |
| 174. | Accurate | 1 | 2* | 3* | 4 | 5** | 6 | 7 | Inaccurate | |

175. What is your major?
  1. Political Science
  2.* History
  3. Sociology
  4. American Civilization
  5.* Communications
  6. Other Social Science
  7. Business-related major
  8. **Other: Art
      Education-Linguistics

176. Year in School?
  1. Freshman
  2.* Sophomore
  3. Junior
  4. Senior
  5.***Graduate student

177. Age: 21*; 27***
178. In national politics, what party do you usually support?
  1. Republican   2.* Democrat   3.* Independent   4. Other:
  5. None**

179. Are you registered to vote? 1.** Yes 2.** No
180. Sex: 1.** Male   2.** Female
181. What is your current living situation;
  1. in the family home
  2. university dorm or apartment
  3.****private apartment
  4. Other

In Deciding Between Two Candidates for an Important Elective Position, a Number of Factors Can Enter Into Your Individual Decision. Please Indicate the Importance to You of Some of These Various Factors.

182. The candidate's personality and style; how he might appear to function under the tensions and stresses of the office.
  Very important       1     2** 3** 4     5     6     7 Not important

183. The candidate's past performance in political office; does he seem to possess the skills required of the office he is aspiring to.
     Very important   1** 2** 3   4   5   6   7 Not important

184. The candidate's party affiliation.
     Very important   1   2   3*  4   5*  6*  7* Not important

185. The candidate's personal history of positions on important issues; how he acted or voted when holding previous public responsibility.
     Very important   1*  2*** 3   4 5   6   7 Not important

186. The candidate's current issue positions.
     Very important   1   2   3** 4   5** 6   7 Not important

187. The current political pressure of the candidate's political party.
     Very important   1   2   3   4   5   6   7 Not important

Answer Items 243-277 Using the Following Answer Codes. Place the Appropriate Number on the Line Provided to the Left of the Item:

1. ABC          2. CBS          3. NBC          4. Don't Know

Referring to the network early evening ("dinner-time") television news broadcasts, in general, which network news program do you thing is . . .

188. _____ . . . . . . the most accurate; NBC****
189. _____ . . . . . . the least accurate? ABC**; Don't Know**
190. _____ . . . . . . the most biased? ABC*; CBS**; Don't Know*
191. _____ . . . . . . the least biased? CBS*; NBC**; Don't Know*
192. _____ . . . . . . the most balanced? NBC****
193. _____ . . . . . . the least balanced? ABC*; CBS*; Don't Know**
194. _____ . . . . . . the most interesting? ABC*; NBC***
195. _____ . . . . . . the least interesting? ABC**; NBC*; Don't Know*

## Indicate Your Personal Evaluation of the Following Public Personalities:
### Dr. Benjamin Spock

| | | 1 | 2 | 3 | 4 | 5 | 6 | 7 | |
|---|---|---|---|---|---|---|---|---|---|
| 196. | Tough | 1 | 2 | 3** | 4** | 5 | 6 | 7 | Soft |
| 197. | Honest | 1 | 2*** | 3* | 4 | 5 | 6 | 7 | Dishonest |
| 198. | Emotional | 1 | 2* | 3** | 4* | 5 | 6 | 7 | Logical |
| 199. | Attractive | 1 | 2 | 3 | 4*** | 5* | 6 | 7 | Unattractive |
| 200. | Strong | 1 | 2 | 3*** | 4* | 5 | 6 | 7 | Weak |
| 201. | Active | 1** | 2** | 3 | 4 | 5 | 6 | 7 | Passive |
| 202. | Clean | 1* | 2*** | 3 | 4 | 5 | 6 | 7 | Dirty |
| 203. | Efficient | 1 | 2 | 3*** | 4 | 5 | 6 | 7 | Bungling |
| 204. | Popular | 1 | 2 | 3** | 4* | 5 | 6* | 7 | Unpopular |
| 205. | Intelligent | 1* | 2*** | 3 | 4 | 5 | 6 | 7 | Unintelligent |
| 206. | Hero | 1 | 2** | 3* | 4* | 5 | 6 | 7 | Villain |
| 207. | Liberal | 1* | 2*** | 3 | 4 | 5 | 6 | 7 | Conservative |
| 208. | Sensitive | 1 | 2*** | 3* | 4 | 5 | 6 | 7 | Insensitive |

## Indicate Your Personal Evaluation of the Following Public Personalities:
### Dr. Henry Kissinger

| | | 1 | 2 | 3 | 4 | 5 | 6 | 7 | |
|---|---|---|---|---|---|---|---|---|---|
| 209. | Tough | 1 | 2** | 3* | 4* | 5 | 6 | 7 | Soft |
| 210. | Honest | 1 | 2 | 3** | 4* | 5* | 6 | 7 | Dishonest |
| 211. | Emotional | 1 | 2* | 3 | 4* | 5 | 6** | 7 | Logical |
| 212. | Attractive | 1 | 2 | 3** | 4* | 5* | 6 | 7 | Unattractive |
| 213. | Strong | 1 | 2* | 3** | 4* | 5 | 6 | 7 | Weak |
| 214. | Active | 1* | 2** | 3* | 4 | 5 | 6 | 7 | Passive |
| 215. | Clean | 1* | 2*** | 3 | 4 | 5 | 6 | 7 | Dirty |
| 216. | Efficient | 1* | 2** | 3* | 4 | 5 | 6 | 7 | Bungling |
| 217. | Popular | 1 | 2 | 3** | 4** | 5 | 6 | 7 | Unpopular |
| 218. | Intelligent | 1** | 2* | 3* | 4 | 5 | 6 | 7 | Unintelligent |
| 219. | Hero | 1 | 2 | 3 | 4*** | 5 | 6* | 7 | Villain |
| 220. | Liberal | 1 | 2 | 3 | 4** | 5** | 6 | 7 | Conservative |
| 221. | Insensitive | 1 | 2 | 3* | 4*** | 5 | 6 | 7 | Insensitive |

## Indicate Your Personal Evaluation of the Following Public Personalities:
### *President Richard Nixon*

| | | | | | | | | |
|---|---|---|---|---|---|---|---|---|
| 222. | Tough | 1 | 2* | 3* | 4** | 5 | 6 | 7 | Soft |
| 223. | Honest | 1 | 2 | 3 | 4* | 5* | 6** | 7 | Dishonest |
| 224. | Emotional | 1 | 2* | 3 | 4* | 5* | 6* | 7 | Logical |
| 225. | Attractive | 1 | 2 | 3 | 4 | 5 | 6*** | 7 | Unattractive |
| 226. | Strong | 1 | 2* | 3 | 4** | 5* | 6 | 7 | Weak |
| 227. | Active | 1 | 2* | 3** | 4 | 5* | 6 | 7 | Passive |
| 228. | Clean | 1* | 2* | 3* | 4* | 5 | 6 | 7 | Dirty |
| 229. | Efficient | 1 | 2 | 3 | 4** | 5* | 6* | 7 | Bungling |
| 230. | Popular | 1 | 2 | 3* | 4* | 5** | 6 | 7 | Unpopular |
| 231. | Intelligent | 1 | 2 | 3** | 4 | 5 | 6* | 7* | Unintelligent |
| 232. | Hero | 1 | 2 | 3 | 4 | 5** | 6* | 7 | Villain |
| 233. | Liberal | 1 | 2 | 3 | 4 | 5 | 6*** | 7* | Conservative |
| 234. | Sensitive | 1 | 2 | 3 | 4* | 5 | 6** | 7* | Insensitive |

## Indicate Your Personal Evaluation of the Following Public Personalities:
### *George McGovern*

| | | | | | | | | |
|---|---|---|---|---|---|---|---|---|
| 235. | Tough | 1 | 2* | 3 | 4** | 5* | 6 | 7 | Soft |
| 236. | Honest | 1 | 2* | 3** | 4* | 5 | 6 | 7 | Dishonest |
| 237. | Emotional | 1 | 2 | 3** | 4* | 5* | 6 | 7 | Logical |
| 238. | Attractive | 1* | 2* | 3* | 4* | 5 | 6 | 7 | Unattractive |
| 239. | Strong | 1 | 2* | 3* | 4** | 5 | 6 | 7 | Weak |
| 240. | Active | 1 | 2** | 3** | 4 | 5 | 6 | 7 | Passive |
| 241. | Clean | 1* | 2*** | 3 | 4 | 5 | 6 | 7 | Dirty |
| 242. | Efficient | 1 | 2 | 3*** | 4* | 5 | 6 | 7 | Bungling |
| 243. | Popular | 1 | 2 | 3**** | 4 | 5 | 6 | 7 | Unpopular |
| 244. | Intelligent | 1* | 2* | 3** | 4 | 5 | 6 | 7 | Unintelligent |
| 245. | Hero | 1 | 2* | 3*** | 4 | 5 | 6 | 7 | Villain |
| 246. | Liberal | 1 | 2** | 3** | 4 | 5 | 6 | 7 | Conservative |
| 247. | Sensitive | 1 | 2** | 3** | 4 | 5 | 6 | 7 | Insensitive |

**Indicate Your Personal Evaluation of the Following Public Personalities:**
*Former Vice President Ky*

| | | | | | | | | | | | | | |
|---|---|---|---|---|---|---|---|---|---|---|---|---|---|
| 248. | Tough | 1** | 2 | | 3* | | 4 | | 5* | 6 | | 7 | Soft |
| 249. | Honest | 1 | 2 | | 3 | | 4** | | 5 | 6* | | 7* | Dishonest |
| 250. | Emotional | 1 | 2 | | 3** | | 4 | | 5* | 6* | | 7 | Logical |
| 251. | Attractive | 1 | 2 | | 3 | | 4*** | | 5* | 6 | | 7 | Unattractive |
| 252. | Strong | 1* | 2* | | 3 | | 4* | | 5* | 6 | | 7 | Weak |
| 253. | Active | 1* | 2 | | 3*** | | 4 | | 5 | 6 | | 7 | Passive |
| 254. | Clean | 1* | 2* | | 3** | | 4 | | 5 | 6 | | 7 | Dirty |
| 255. | Efficient | 1 | 2 | | 3* | | 4** | | 5 | 6* | | 7 | Bungling |
| 256. | Popular | 1 | 2 | | 3* | | 4* | | 5** | 6 | | 7 | Unpopular |
| 257. | Intelligent | 1 | 2* | | 3* | | 4* | | 5* | 6 | | 7 | Unintelligent |
| 258. | Hero | 1 | 2 | | 3 | | 4** | | 5** | 6 | | 7 | Villain |
| 259. | Liberal | 1 | 2 | | 3 | | 4** | | 5 | 6* | | 7* | Conservative |
| 260. | Sensitive | 1 | 2 | | 3 | | 4** | | 5* | 6* | | 7 | Insensitive |

Issue Identification: Answer the Following Questions in One or Two Sentences.

(1) What organization did Daniel Ellsberg work for which put him in a position to gain access to the "Pentagon Papers"? (2)*

(2) Who is Wilbur Mills? (2)

(3) Where in Vietnam is An Loc?

(4) Who is Willie Brandt? (2)

(5) What is "strip mining"? (3)

(6) What network produced "The Selling of the Pentagon"? (2)

(7) Who is Theodore White? (2)

(8) Where was Martin Luther King assassinated and by whom? (1)

(9) Who is Terry Sanford? (2)

(10) Who is the President of Chile? (3)

(11) Who is Germain Greer? What did she write? (4)

(12) Who was Samuel Gompers? (2)

(13) Who was Henry Wallace? (2)

(14) What do the acronyms "MOS" and "MAG" mean to you? (0)

(15) Define "lip flap" and "reverses." (0)

*Number of Correct Responses

# Notes

# Notes

## Chapter 1
## Politics and Communication

1. Inferences from these data, the social implications of patterns detected, and predicted outcomes in terms of either mass value change or changing political agendas must be (and are) kept analytically separate from the message analysis.

2. One is reminded of the oft-quoted definition of news given by David Brinkley: "News is what I say it is. It's something worth knowing by my standards." Interview in *TV Guide*, April 11, 1964. See also W. Geiber, "News is What Newspapermen Make It," in L.A. Dexter and D.M. White (eds.), *People, Society, and Mass Communications* (New York: Free Press, 1964), pp. 173-82. Another working definition of "news" might include the news characteristic of "uniqueness," i.e., the "out-of-the ordinary" nature of the story being reported.

3. B.H. Bagdikian, *The Information Machines* (New York: Harper & Row, 1971), p. xii.

4. D.M. White, "The Gatekeeper: A Case Study in the Selection of News," *Journalism Quarterly* 27, no. 4 (Fall 1950), 383-90.

5. M. Novak, "The Inevitable Bias of Television," in M. Barrett (ed.), *Survey of Broadcast Journalism, 1970-1971* (New York: Grosset and Dunlap, 1971), pp. 121-32.

6. Themistocles had propaganda messages, "news" about his armies, engraved on stones at watering places which he knew the opposing Ionian fleet would visit. Alexander the Great developed the first "wire service" explicitly established to influence domestic opinion concerning a specific military venture. A series of runners from Persia to Macedonia, carried news of Alexander's exploits back to the homeland. A Holy Roman Emperor of the thirteenth century, Frederick II, improved upon Alexander's techniques by developing a "multi-channel" news message. Frederick employed a staff of "public relations experts" who produced a stream of documents which supported the Emperor in his struggles with the Pope. These highly sophisticated communications were constructed so as to be most effective when read aloud (which was important in an era of high citizen illiteracy). Full use was made of rhetorical and poetic devices such as repetition, contrast, rhyme and alliteration to facilitate easy remembrance. Furthermore, Frederick mobilized large numbers of troubadors who carried his "news" in lyrical form throughout the Holy Roman Empire. During the Thirty Years' War, when the coach of Frederick of the Palatine that was carrying chancellory records fell into the hands of the Holy Roman Emperor, the latter immediately published these documents throughout the Empire. Likewise, when secret papers concerning negotiations between the

Emperor and the King of Spain fell into the hands of the Protestants, these were published as "news" throughout the Protestant strongholds of Europe. Cited in W.P. Davison, "Some Trends in International Propaganda," *The Annals of the American Academy of Political and Social Science*, 398 (1971), 1-13. On historical material and perspective, also see G. Gerbner, "Mass Media and Human Communication Theory," in F.X. Dance (ed.), *Human Communication Theory: Original Essays* (New York: Holt, Rinehart & Winston, 1967).

7. James Farley had to send questionnaires to loyal Democrats throughout the state to ascertain the quality of reception from various local stations. Cited in J.M. Burns, *Roosevelt: The Lion and the Fox* (New York: Harcourt, Brace, and World, 1956), p. 118.

8. See L.W. Pye (ed.), *Communications and Political Development* (Princeton: Princeton University Press, 1963); W.P. Davison, *International Political Communication* (New York: Praeger, 1965); W. Schramm, *Mass Media and National Development* (Stanford University Press, 1964). The classic example remains Ataturk's propulsion of Turkey into the twentieth century. Ataturk invented the concept of *Halk-evleri* or "Peoples' Houses," communal places throughout Turkey where the villagers could gather to discuss social and political issues. Ataturk then installed radios in each of the Peoples' Houses which he had built and then decided what political news and views would and would not be broadcast over the radios. Cited in D. Lerner, *The Passing of Traditional Society* (Glencoe: Free Press, 1958), esp. pp. 62-65.

9. This assertion can be tested empirically. Variables such as the extent of media use, reliance on media, and motivational bases for political behavior of individuals within a given system must be assessed in order to test the empirical validity of this statement.

10. One wonders if it is only an unarticulated notion among scholars that Western man is somehow more modern, more intelligent, and more media-sophisticated (and therefore immune to media effects), or if there in fact exist real social-structural-psychological characteristics of the Third World media-milieu which render these environments qualitatively more susceptible to mass media influences than Western, modern societies.

11. One possible policy implication of the two-step flow, as conceived, is to downplay the necessity of government control, supervision, or interest in TV news per se because the theory argues that the information brokers, and not the television news, are the source of attitude change and reinforcement.

12. People are not compelled to *use* the media at their disposal; thus one must question the *use* of the media and not the *effect* of the media (as a causal agent), the effect being secondary to the use and therefore much less powerful both in fact and as an explanatory paradigm.

13. I. de S. Pool, "TV: A New Dimension in Politics," in E. Burdick and A.J. Brodbeck (eds.), *American Voting Behavior* (Glencoe: Ill.: Free Press, 1959), 197-208.

14. For a review of the literature, see W. Weiss, "Effects of the Mass Media of Communication," in G. Lindzey and E. Aronson (eds.), *The Handbook of Social Psychology*, vol. 5 (2nd ed.) (Reading, Mass.: Addison-Wesley, 1968), pp. 156-61.

15. J.G. Blumer and D. McQuail, *Television in Politics* (Chicago: University of Chicago Press, 1969).

16. P.F. Lazarsfeld, B. Berelson and H. Gaudet, *The People's Choice* (New York: Columbia University Press, 1948); E. Katz and P.F. Lazarsfeld, *Personal Influence* (Glencoe, Ill.: Free Press, 1955); E. Katz, "The Two-Step Flow of Communication," *Public Opinion Quarterly* 21 (1957), 61-78.

17. F.H. Knower, "Experimental Studies of Changes in Attitude: I. A Study of the Effect of Oral Argument on Changes of Attitude," *Journal of Social Psychology* 6 (1935), 315-47; F.H. Knower, "Experimental Studies of Changes in Attitude: II. A Study of the Effect of Printed Argument on Changes in Attitude," *Journal of Abnormal and Social Psychology* 30 (1936), 522-32; W.H. Wilke, "An Experimental Comparison of the Speech, the Radio, and the Printed Page as Propaganda Devices," *Archives of Psychology* New York, no. 169, 1934.

18. R.K. Merton, *Mass Persuasion: The Social Psychology of a War Bond Drive* (New York: Harper, 1946).

19. B.S. Greenberg, "Dimensions of Informal Communication," in W.A. Danielson (ed.), *Paul J. Deutschmann Memorial Papers in Mass Communications Research* (Cincinnati: Scripps-Howard Research, 1963), 35-43.

20. B. Berelson, P.F. Lazarsfeld, and W.N. McPhee, *Voting* (Chicago: University of Chicago Press, 1954).

21. D.C. Miller, "A Research Note on Mass Communications," *American Sociological Review* 10 (1945), 691-94.

22. R.J. Hill and C.M. Bonjean, "News Diffusion: A Test of the Regularity Hypothesis," *Journalism Quarterly* 41 (1964), 336-42.

23. B.S. Greenberg, "Person-to-Person Communication in the Diffusion of News Events," *Journalism Quarterly* 41 (1964), 489-94.

24. S. Feshbach and R. Singer, *Television and Aggression* (San Francisco: Jossey-Bass, 1971), 158; see also "A Ten Year View of Public Attitudes Toward Television and Other Mass Media, 1959-1968," a report by Roper Research Associates.

25. K. Lewin, "Studies in Group Decision," in D. Cartwright and A. Zander (eds.), *Group Dynamics* (Evanston: Row, Peterson, 1953), 287-301; E.B. Bennett, "Discussion, Decision, Commitment, and Consensus in 'Group Decision,'" *Human Relations* 8 (1955), 251-73; UNESCO, *Rural Television in Japan* (Paris: UNESCO, 1960).

26. G.E. and K. Lang, "The Inferential Structure of Political Communications: A Study in Unwitting Bias," *Public Opinion Quarterly* 19 (1955), 168-83; Lang & Lang, "The Unique Perspective of Television and Its Effect: A Pilot Study," in W. Schramm (ed.), *Mass Communications* (Urbana: University of Illinois Press, 1960), 544-60.

27. J. Trenaman and D. McQuail, *Television and the Political Image* (London: Methuen, 1961).

28. S. Kelley, *Professional Public Relations and Political Power* (Baltimore: Johns Hopkins Press, 1956).

29. Hill and Bonjean, "News Diffusion."

30. Greenberg, "Person-to-Person Communication," pp. 489-94.

31. "Highly important information" would include such events as the assassination of a president, a declaration of war, and a major airplane crash; "relatively unimportant events" are happenings such as the release of a new record album, changes in clothing styles, and personal-interest type stories; "moderately important information" includes such events as the passing of a bill, current unemployment rates, the appointment of a new ambassador, and so forth.

32. W. Weiss, "Effects of the Mass Media of Communication," in G. Lindzey and E. Aronson (eds.), *The Handbook of Social Psychology* 2nd ed., 5 vols. (Reading, Mass.: Addison-Wesley, 1968), 5, 77-195.

33. V.C. Troldahl and R. Van Dam, "Face to Face Communication about Major Topics in the News." quoted with permission, *Public Opinion Quarterly* 29 (1965), 634.

34. J.B. Martin, *Overtaken by Events* (New York: Doubleday, 1966), pp. 398, 399. Copyright © 1966 by John Bartlow Martin. Reprinted by permission of Doubleday & Company, Inc.

35. For example, the 1963 Iraqi revolution, where the mutilated body of Premier Abdul Karim Kassem was dragged into the studio and shown to the audience. M. Mayer, *About Television* (New York: Harper and Row, 1972), p. 244. In some cases such vividness can be a political disadvantage to those who wish to mask the true importance of their political resources. One of the powers of radio as a revolutionary weapon, for example, lies in the fact that a small group of men who successfully capture a government radio station can describe events and claim a revolutionary following which in fact does not at that time exsit. Thus political mobilization can be accomplished on the strength of described political resources which exist only in the imaginations of a small revolutionary group.

36. R.J. Youman, "What Does America Think Now?" *TV Guide*, September 30, 1972.

37. In terms of mass unrest and anomic rioting, not only does television afford a rapid form of communication which can leave the authorities unprepared to meet political demands, it also communicates over extended periods of time various portrayals of "better lives" which leads to mounting latent unrest which can be ignited by "newsworthy events" such as the King assassination. As Wedge notes: "The penetration of vast quantities of appeal and views of better material life into the living rooms of the American poor via television has stirred expectations and frustration; it is not accidental that television sets have been the particular targets of looters in urban riots" (pp. 40-41). From B. Wedge,

"International Propaganda and Statecraft," *The Annals of the American Academy of Political and Social Science*, 398, (1971), 36-43. Other examples of bypassing governmental information gatekeepers would be the live coverage of the killing of Oswald, the terrorism at the 1972 Summer Olympics in Munich, and the assassination of Robert Kennedy.

38. Pre-Columbians had a series of signals which stretched from the tip of South America to the jungles of Central America, as did businessmen in America in the early nineteenth century between New York and Philadelphia (to send priority stock-market quotations), yet the primitive and restricted nature of the signals which could be sent using these methods rules these forms out as true commercial channels of involved communication. Until the invention of the telegraph, the fastest form of long-distance communication was the running horse, and the fastest of all horse-based long-distance communication, the Pony Express, transmitted messages at speeds of only five miles an hour over the route from St. Joseph, Missouri to Sacramento, California. The development of telegraph, telephone, and radio communication drastically reduced this transit time, but until recently, the communication of the powerful vivid components of a message, that is, film, still entailed a loss in the speed of communication. Until the relatively recent development of magnetic videotape, film from fast-breaking overseas news stories had to be flown by plane to New York, where squads of messengers on motorcycles would rush the film from La Guardia Airport over the streets of New York City to have the film processed and then delivered to the news studios.

39. Although in a related sense, the international sharing of the geostatic orbit and/or satellite communications hardware (or the lack of international cooperation) can include and exclude nations from certain forms of international communication, much as the ability to "jam" fixed and mobile terrestial communication did in the past. See the Twentieth Century Fund, *The Future of Satellite Communications* (New York: The Twentieth Century Fund, 1970).

40. F. Friendly, *Due to Circumstances Beyond Our Control . . .* (New York: Random House Vintage Press, 1967), p. 95.

41. It took Lord Nelson eleven minutes to display the flags at Trafalgar that read, "England expects every man to do his duty."

42. Bagdikian, *Information Machines*, p. 95.

43. The present complexity and size of the necessary encoding equipment in many cases makes electronic journalism somewhat ill-suited to cover totally unexpected and fast-breaking news as well as a highly mobile print reporter who can get the story, file it, and have his story quickly appear in print journalism sources.

44. J.T. Klapper, "What We Know About the Effects of Mass Communication: The Brink of Hope," *Public Opinion Quarterly* 21, 453-74, reprinted in A.G. Smith (ed.), *Communication and Culture* (New York: Holt, Rinehart and Winston, 1966), p. 538.

45. F.C. White, "Balancing the Campaign," in R. Hiebert, R. Jones, E.

Lotito, and J. Lorenz, *Political Image Merchants* (Washington, D.C.: Acropolis Press, 1971), p. 59.

46. E. Chester, *Radio, Television and American Politics* (New York: Sheer and Ward, 1969), p. 18.

47. J. McGinniss, *The Selling of the President, 1968* (New York: Trident Press, 1969).

48. D. Nimmo, *The Political Persuaders* (Englewood Cliffs, N.J.: Prentice-Hall, 1970).

49. K. and G. Lang, "The Unique Perspective of Television and its Effect," *American Sociological Review* 18, no. 1 (1953), 3-12; Lang and Lang, *Politics and Television* (Chicago: Quadrangle, 1968), esp. pp. 11-77.

50. The problem, and home videotape machines may change this situation, is that unlike print news which can be read at any time at the convenience of the user, television news must be watched at the time of broadcast. Thus pressure exists to make the news as "entertaining" as possible in order to insure that the audience will "tune in" at the given news hour. R. MacNeil, *The People Machine* (New York: Harper and Row, 1968), pp. 40-55.

51. H. Mendelsohn and I. Crespi, *Polls, Television and the New Politics* (Scranton, Pa.: Chandler, 1970), p. 301.

52. Nimmo, *Political Persuaders*, p. 155.

53. Cited in B. Rubin, *Political Television* (Belmont, Calif.: Wadsworth, 1967), p. 130.

54. W. Small, *Political Power and the Press* (New York: W.W. Norton, 1972), pp. 383-84 and passim.

55. Cited in A. Schlesinger, Jr., *A Thousand Days* (Greenwich, Conn.: Fawcett Crest, 1965), p. 73.

## Chapter 2
## Developing Techniques of Television
## Content Analysis

1. N.E. Cutler and E.S. Cutler, "The West European USIA Macro-Survey: A Tool for Cross-time/Cross-national Comparative Analysis," paper delivered at the Annual Meeting of the International Studies Association, San Juan, March 1971; N.E. Cutler, E.S. Cutler, and F. Lavipour, "Mass and Elite Attitudes toward the Europeanization of West European Security and Defense," in *European Security in the Age of U.S.-Soviet Strategic Parity* (Philadelphia: Foreign Policy Research Institute, 1970).

2. G. Almond, *The American People and Foreign Policy* (New York: Harcourt, Brace: 1950); J. Rosenau, "The Attentive Public and Foreign Policy" (Center of International Studies, Princeton University, March 1968); J.E. Muller, "Presidential Popularity from Truman to Johnson," *American Political Science Review* 64 (1970).

3. R.W. Cobb and C.D. Elder, *Participation in American Politics: The Dynamics of Agenda-Building* (Boston: Allyn and Bacon, 1972), p. 141.

4. M. Lipsky, "Protest as a Political Resource," *American Political Science Review* 62 (1968), 1151-53.

5. N. Long, "The Local Community as an Ecology of Games," *American Journal of Sociology* 44 (1958), 260.

6. B. Bagdikian, *The Information Machines* (New York: Harper and Row, 1971), p. 90.

7. It must be noted that in the case of the United States news format, where the commercial aspect of the news broadcast permeates the entire news format, there is a somewhat greater tendency for television as a medium to preempt regular commercial broadcasting for "newsworthy" issue and event coverage.

8. Cobb and Elder, *Participation in American Politics*, pp. 135 ff.

9. G. Stempel, "The Prestige Press Covers the 1960 Presidential Campaign," *Journalism Quarterly* 38 (1961), 157-63.

10. E. Efron, *The News Twisters* (Los Angeles: Nash, 1970).

11. L.W. Sargent, "Communicator Image and News Reception," *Journalism Quarterly* 42 (1965), 35-44.

12. N.E. Cutler, A.S. Tedesco, and R.S. Frank, *The Differential Encoding of Political Images* (Philadelphia: Foreign Policy Research Institute, 1972).

13. For a review of this literature, see R.S. Frank, "Non-textual Psychopolitical Assessment: A Multi-Method Approach to Elite Analysis," in M.G. Herman and T. Milburn (eds.), *A Psychological Examination of Political Man* (forthcoming, 1973), and idem., "Biological Referents in Political Rhetoric: A Study in Verbal Kinesics," paper to be presented at the Ninth World Congress, International Political Science Association, Montreal, August 1973.

14. Cutler, Tedesco, and Frank, *Differential Encoding*, pp. 197 ff.

15. Ibid., pp. 264 ff.

16. We must expect such behavioral differences because both the psycholinguistic verbal manifestations of personality traits and the nonverbal manifestations of personality traits are generally assumed in the relevant literature to be nonconscious and not amenable to personal behavioral manipulations. Thus the very humanness of the newscasters generates a series of cues which are transmitted nonconsciously, even if these cues are differentially received and acted upon by different audience-types.

17. For a review of the literature that reports the relative persuasive weight of nonverbal as opposed to verbal communication, see A.T. Dittmann, *Interpersonal Messages of Emotion* (New York: Springer, 1972), and A. Mehrabian, *Silent Messages* (Belmont, Calif.: Wadsworth, 1971).

18. In Appendix B, asterisks are presented next to possible responses to signify the frequency and distribution of responses to specific questions. No internal distinctions are made within the aggregated totals. This not only

guarantees a certain degree of desired anonymity, the frequent reassignment of coders into different coding teams renders the data produced as something akin to the product of a "group mind." Thus the simple presentation of aggregated questionnaire responses is deemed appropriate.

19. K. Krippendorff, "Reliability of Recording Instructions: Multivariate Agreement for Nominal Data," *Behavioral Science* 16 (1971), 228-235.

20. R. Frank, "Strategies and Issues in Content Analysis," unpublished paper, Foreign Policy Research Institute, 1973.

21. July sample broadcasts were taped by the Vanderbilt Archive and then dubbed to 1/2" tape. All coding was conducted using 1/2" videotape monitor screens, thus controlling for size of image.

22. A partial preemption of one October broadcast compelled to dump all data for that day and include instead the following Monday of the next week. Thus our three week-sample took us through election eve.

## Chapter 3
## Network News Coverage of the 1972 Presidential
## Election Campaign Period: A Review of the Data

1. The relative frequency-placement score ranges from approaching zero to "1.00," with the lower score representing an "earlier" mean placement in the storyboard lineup.

2. O.R. Holsti, *Content Analysis for the Social Sciences and Humanities* (Reading, Mass.: Addison-Wesley, 1969), p. 140.

3. Note the number of people who believed in the "invasion from Mars" simply because they heard so much about it on Welles' program. Many of them were people who first doubted the authenticity of the story. H. Cantril, *The Invasion from Mars* (New York: Harper Torchbooks, 1969 ed.).

4. See especially C.I. Hoviland, et al., *The Order of Presentation in Persuasion* (New Haven: Yale University Press, 1956) and for a more recent review, W. Wilson and H. Miller, "Repetition, Order of Presentation, and Timing of Arguments and Measures as Determinants of Opinion Change," *Journal of Personality and Social Psychology* 9 (1968), 184-88.

5. P.H. Tannenbaum, "Effect of Serial Position on Recall of Radio News Stories," *Journalism Quarterly* 31 (1954), 319-23.

6. M. Green, *Television News: Anatomy and Process* (Belmont, Calif.: Wadsworth, 1969), pp. 236-53.

7. Sloan Commission, *On the Cable: The Television of Abundance* (New York: McGraw-Hill, 1971), pp. 120-22.

8. This "unbalance" of course exists for a series of valid reasons and unavoidable news-gathering and marketing constraints.

9. See S. Eisenstein, *Film Form and Film Sense* (New York: Meridian Books, 1957 ed.). Also R. Spottiswoode, *A Grammar of the Film* (Berkeley: University of California Press, 1950 ed.).

10. R.S. Frank, "Electronic Folklore," in D.C. Schwartz (ed.), *Folklore and Politics* (in preparation).

11. E. Chester, *Radio, Television and American Politics* (New York: Sheer and Ward, 1969).

12. See W. DeVries, "Taking the Voter's Pulse," in R. Hiebert, R. Jones, E. Lotito, and J. Lorenz (eds.), *The Political Image Merchants* (Washington, D.C.: Acropolis, 1971), pp. 71-72.

13. C. Osgood, et al., *The Measurement of Meaning* (Urbana: University of Illinois Press, 1957).

14. Liberal and conservative can be defined according to general underlying philosophies and/or in terms of positions on specific issues which the liberal or conservative assumes. The major philosophical dispute between liberals and conservatives can be identified with the antithesis of free will and determinism, of utopia and reality. The liberal tends to be utopian, he believes in the perfectability of man and in the possibility of forging solutions to all of man's social problems. The conservative is a "realist," he believes in the imperfectability of man and in the impossibility of forging solutions to all of man's social problems. From these two philosophically opposite approaches to the realities of the world, come very different policy positions on different issues. The liberal tends to favor innovations, the conservative is from Missouri—he wants the validity of new approaches validated. It is in terms of some of these specific policy positions taken by persons considered to be liberal or conservative that we have dichotomized liberal and conservative.

15. N.E. Cutler, A.S. Tedesco, and R.S. Frank, *The Differential Encoding of Network Television News* (Philadelphia: Foreign Policy Research Institute, 1972).

16. Gallup data taken from Gallup Opinion Index, October 1972 (#88).

17. For general reviews of this methodology, see D. Campbell, "From Description to Experimentation: Interpreting Trends as Quasi-Experiments," in C. Harris (ed.), *Problems in Measuring Change* (Madison: University of Wisconsin Press, 1963); T.R. Gurr, *Politimetrics* (Englewood Cliffs, N.J.: Prentice-Hall, 1972), pp. 141-70.

18. Taking each issue separately, all of which had two of three possible matches, the probability for each issue of matching at least two network trends with Gallup response trends = 0.5. The cumulative probability of achieving at least two matches on all six issues, therefore, is $(0.5)^6(2) = H_0 = 0.03125$.

## Conclusion

1. Meadow has shown the differences in coverage which can be attributed to "proxies" to be minimal. A more interesting question would focus on who these proxies are. Can we say, for example, that Wright Patman holding hearings on the Watergate incident was acting as a proxy for McGovern? More important-

ly, does the audience link the proxy with the candidate? We must also consider proxies to be important to the candidates' strategies, since they may serve to demonstrate party unity or perpetuate the image of an incumbent as too occupied with the affairs of state to campaign. Finally, we may wish to consider whether it is the candidate who benefits or the proxy himself from proxy campaigns, since the proxy gains public exposure (at party expense) which may be useful for his own political ambitions. See R. Meadow, "A Cross Media Comparison of News Coverage During the 1972 Presidential Campaign," *Journalism Quarterly* (forthcoming, 1973).

2. Our analysis of the *New York Times* furthermore shows many similarities with television news coverage. Of course, the reader must decide for himself whether the *Times* is "biased."

3. M. Klein and N. Maccoby, "Newspaper Objectivity in the 1952 Campaign," *Journalism Quarterly* 31, no. 3 (1954), 285-96.

4. Meadow, "Cross-Media Comparison."

5. Given the general importance of most of the stories covered, it seems impossible that such a difference between objective "news gathering" levels and amount of reporting could exist. One might want to argue that CBS is "biased" against "hard news" since of the three networks, CBS devoted the most time to soft news, but this line of reasoning does not get us very far. Television as an institution is itself "biased" against news coverage in general in that only twenty-odd minutes of national network news coverage per night per network is programmed. By the same token, however, it could be argued that the television audience is "biased" against the reception of news by the fact that "news magazine" programs generally do not do very well in the Nielsen ratings and in other similar television-watching indicators.

6. This power is, of course, also a function of the credibility of the media, the availability of the medium in question, and alternative sources of information.

7. (Switched referring to the two-way communication process such as telephones as opposed to one-way communication such as contemporary television; radio talk shows are a classic example of the evolution of a nonswitched medium becoming a switched medium.)


## Appendix A
## Television News-Coding Protocol

1. For example, in coding "crowd coverage" the coders had to both ascertain the size and the "friendliness" of the crowd, a two-step decision which allowed for multiplicative error at both steps.

# Index

# Index

# About the Author

**Robert Shelby Frank** is currently a Research Associate and the Research Coordinator for the Political Communications Research Group of the Foreign Policy Research Institute, Philadelphia, Pennsylvania. Dr. Frank received the B.A. from the University of Notre Dame in 1967, the M.A. from the University of Pennsylvania in 1969, and the Ph.D. from the University of Pennsylvania in 1972. In addition, Dr. Frank has completed a course of studies in Salzburg, Austria on European politics and has recently completed a year of post-doctoral research as a Post-doctoral Fellow in the Psychology and Politics Program at Yale University.

Dr. Frank has conducted extensive research in a number of politics and communication areas. His Ph.D. dissertation investigated the political rhetoric of Presidents of the United States and Dr. Frank has conducted a series of studies of non-verbal behavior of political elites using mass media broadcast data. Currently Dr. Frank is collaborating with a number of European and American scholars who are interested in cross-national politics and media research. In addition, Dr. Frank has recently been awarded a National Institute of Education research grant to investigate the relative effects of television news and classroom curriculum material upon the political socialization process of school children.